THEY SHALL SEE GOD

Charleston, SC
www.PalmettoPublishing.com

They Shall See God
Copyright © 2022 by Bryan Kaiser

First Edition

Paperback: 979-8-88590-641-8
eBook: 979-8-88590-640-1

THEY SHALL SEE GOD

Eyeglasses, evangelism, and a
mission to serve the poor.

BRYAN KAISER

PRAISE FOR THEY SHALL SEE GOD

"As someone who reads more than 100 books a year, this is a must read. It's so compelling that I could not put it down. It will make you laugh, break your heart and heal again with the wonderful stories of people of all ages being given the gift of sight and leading lost souls to Christ. As a believer it has affected my life in a very positive way. Before reading this book other than praying for the less fortunate of God's children and donations to various organizations I didn't give it a lot of thought. I now know how very blessed I am and I want to do more for those in need. After meeting Bryan and visiting the God's Eyes headquarters, realized that he is a true man of God. Bryan is a true evangelist traveling to the most underdeveloped locations around the world giving sight to those who would otherwise never see and guiding the poor to salvation."

-Elaine Erwin
Fayetteville, Georgia

"I met Bryan Kaiser in 2008. I have been on 1 or 2 mission trips nearly every year since then with him. I have read the book and I am personally aware of many of the stories that he shares. We have both been on a journey that has seen each of us grow in our spiritual life. We both had come from conservative Christian backgrounds and God revealed a whole new world to us. We saw God do miracles and we saw attacks from Satan. Through the stories that Bryan shares, you will be able to see the heart of God. I would encourage you to read the book and let God change your life even as he has changed ours."

-Eddie Moore, M.D.
Abilene, Texas

"Just imagine you are in a village high up in the Andes in Peru with a 12 year old deaf mute girl, who sees nothing clearly because she has never had access to get the prescription glasses she needs. Now imagine the most beautiful and unforgettable smile you have ever seen on her face when she has her first proper prescription eyewear placed on her face by a God's Eyes team member. This, my friends, is the real heart and soul of the God's Eyes ministry. I have been so honored to serve with Bryan on ten God's Eyes medical mission trips and this is just one of hundreds of amazing stories in bringing vision to others in just my time with him in the name of Jesus. Bryan and I worked closely together in our private practice for nearly twenty years and his heart and optical talents are second to none. His ministry in God's Eyes is so amazing in helping to serve some of the 2+ billion people on earth who don't see well because of having no access to vision care, the leading cause of poor vision. May many continue to be led to Jesus in Bryan's incredible ministry at God's Eyes!"

-Scott A Bowser, OD, retired Founder & CEO,
Peachtree City Eye Center Atlanta, GA

❝We have worked with God's eyes and founder Bryan Kaiser in Ecuador over the last 5 years. We love the focus on not only meeting people's physical needs but also making sure their spiritual needs receive equal attention. After around 5 years of praying for a man in our town, God's Eyes held a clinic and one more time shared the gospel with our friend. After having received his glasses and going to a "prayer room" our friend surrendered to Jesus! Thank you so much for all the hard work you guys do to make such events possible!"

-Andy & Priscilla DVarga, Acts 1:8 Mission Society
San Pedro, Ecuador

❝I was drawn to the book 'They Shall See God" by Bryan Kaiser because I love a good story, whether it's a biography or nonfiction. I want to hear the good, the bad, and the ugly of real life from real people. Kaiser weaves his tales of God's Eyes ministry, surprisingly without the saccharin-sweet I've come to expect from many faith-based books. It was raw and real and even ugly at times, but also so authentic and so readable. I stayed up till 3 a.m. and read it in one sitting. I laughed out loud at some of the pickles they got into, and shed tears over the horrid conditions many experience outside of our white-bread world. I was challenged, inspired, happy, glad, rejoicing, devastated, praising

God from page one until the end. It's a grand tale and one that will make you think. Some of the stories impacted my heart and still come to mind well after I put the book down. I highly recommend taking the time to sit with Mr. Kaiser's book and soak it in. It's worth your time."

-Dana Chitwood MS, AFC®

Peachtree City, Georgia

"It is a wonderful book of how God is at work in our lives, leading, guiding, growing and transforming the lives of those willing to respond to His call. It is full of beautiful stories of how God led the author to give up his plan for his life and follow His plan resulting in the transformation of thousands of lives in many parts of the world. It is an easy read with wonderful stories of God at work, gradually bringing the author to trust the Lord completely with God's plan for his life. You will be inspired and encouraged to seek Him in your own life."

-Ron Collins, International Friendship Ministries Inc.

Columbus, Georgia

"They Shall See God" is nourishment for the soul. Bryan does a masterful job captivating the reader's attention and then taking you on a journey that inspires, evokes heartfelt joy and sadness, and provides poignant reminders of how blessed and thankful we should all feel to live in the United States. I had a very hard time putting this book down because of how relatable, emotionally provoking, and genuinely interesting Bryan's stories were. This memoir reminds us as Christians that the Lord works in mysterious and glorious ways, and if we can just suspend our desire to control, He will make things fall in place. Bryan doesn't just let God drive the car; he hands Him the keys and gets in the back seat. This level of devotion, trust, and acknowledgment of the Lord's plan for us is nothing short of awe-inspiring. If you'd like to be reminded of what it means to follow Jesus and truly love thy neighbor then I strongly suggest you read this amazing book."

-Alex De los Reyes, Biomedical National Sales Director

Sharpsburg, Georgia

"This book is phenomenal!! I was enthralled and loved every minute of it. Bryan is so honest and funny while telling of the amazing stories and miracles of our magnificent God. He perfectly depicts the struggle of letting go of the known and our comforts to follow God. He highlights how the leap of faith is scary, but in the end better than anything we could have imagined. This book reveals what being a follower of Christ looks like and the beautiful and crazy adventures God has for us while He uses us to bring His good news to the ends of the Earth. This book has inspired me to listen to God's voice in my own life; trusting that He has something for me that I can't even imagine! A must read book!"

-Jamie Jones, Broker and Owner Paraclete Realty
Bozeman, Montana

"In 2013, I went on my 1st Mission Trip to Ecuador. The 1st evening, my wife and I sat down at the dinner table with Bryan. He wrecked our life with his testimonies and stories about how God changed his life and put him on his journey leading God's Eyes. Last year, July 2021, we went on our 6th Mission Trip with him to Ecuador and he told us he was writing a book about his life and many of his trips. Then about February of this year, he sent my wife and I a copy to read. We could not put it down as we read of how God is working through Bryan and his teams. Several of the stories he wrote were about trips that we were there with him in Ecuador. The Chapter, Stay With Me, really touched me and made me realize that I am guilty of mainly asking God to help when I really need something. It made me want to depend on Him under all circumstances and praise Him when things are going good as well as when things are not so good. The last chapter especially is so uplifting. I have read it at least 3 times and every time it brings tears to my eyes. I truly want to learn to see everything though God's Eyes."

-Ray Henicke, Pharmacist
Abielne, Texas

"The story of God's Eyes is an amazing and inspirational testimony to what God will do through believers when we surrender our will and follow His leading. Bryan Kaiser vividly describes the conditions of many in the world who suffer the hardships of extreme poverty in undeveloped countries. He inspires us through his experiences to do more, love deeper, and give generously to share the Gospel and mitigate the suffering."

-Luci Hough, Executive Director
Fayette Pregnancy Resource Center
Fayetteville, Georgia

"They Shall See God is first and foremost a story of the love God has for the poor. It is also the story of Bryan Kaiser who blindly followed God's plan leading him to some of the poorest slum cities in the world while facing insurmountable odds to bring sight to the poor. One man with a clear vision of what God asked him to do led to a life filled with experiences that most of us will never have. I had a hard time putting this book down. I loved sharing some of these stories with my granddaughter. I am sure you will be telling them to your children before long as well."

-David A. Scott, President Scott Properties (Retired)
San Juan Capistrano, California

ACKNOWLEDGEMENTS

For the past sixteen years, God's Eyes has held eye clinics in over 400 villages throughout the world. We have brought vision and the love of Jesus to the world through well over 100 mission trips.

This journey continues to be a transforming adventure I had not planned, but God had. We have served in mountain villages at 18,000 feet above sea level, far above the cloud line and we have served in garbage dumps all around the globe. Any place in the world where the poor are, there is a need for vision and hope. God's Eyes wants to be there.

I used to think that around 10 percent of the people in the world were poor. Now I believe that 10 percent of the world lives like most of us in America and that the rest of the world is poor. I've read statistics that state that 56 percent of the people on this planet survive on less than $2 per day. In many of the villages where we have served, some of the people eke daily life on far less than that. It's one thing to hear about this on television or read about poverty in the third world, but until you enter that world you will never grasp the extent of the hardships associated with it.

I am exceedingly grateful to all those who have been a part of this journey with me. To Father, His Son, and His Holy Spirit for guiding me lovingly and patiently through every step I've taken on this journey.

To my wife, Jennifer, for all her unending love and support, who made this all possible by encouraging me to leap when I wanted to retreat. To my son, Drew, his wife Janelle and my daughters Ashley and Taylor whom I love dearly and miss greatly every time I leave on my travels. To my grandchildren, Kellan, Arlington, Wilde, and the ones still to come with whom I wanted to share my stories. To all my dear friends including Woody, Mark, and Ken who never grew weary of their task to get me to write this book. To Fred who has spent hundreds of hours rewriting this book with me and to Claudia and Carolyn and Drew for helping to edit this book.

To all the amazing God's Eyes volunteers, all the missionaries, churches, and mission organizations who partnered in the field with us. I am deeply grateful to you all. Special thanks from the bottom of my heart to all the wonderful generous donors who have enabled us to do what we do. And of course, to the poor who have taught me what joy is while enduring life with extreme lack of provisions and what real faith looks like while living under such difficult circumstances.

CONTENTS

Stranger in a Strange Land 1

The Beginning 4

Thanks, Jenn! 7

The Convention 10

Taking Baby Steps 15

Meeting Valerie 21

Mud Cookies and
Other "Delights" 29

The Leap 39

Dress For Success 44

Marta 49

A Recurring Temptation 57

Zambia 62

Setting Up Shop 71

Time to Grow Up 76

That's Not Necessary 78

Just Ask Me 85

Who Hung Lights in the Sky? . 88

A Punch in the Face 92

An Early Year in Retrospect . . . 95

The Joy of Kidney Stones 99

How Did That Happen? 102

Miracle in the Closet 107

Looking the Other Way 109

Critters and Crappy Places . . . 112

The Hug 123

Voodoo Child 125

Hard to Believe 128

Down the Drain 131

Brother, Can You
Spare a Fork? 134

A Heartfelt Matter 136

Mozambique 139

Letter to Dad 145

A Great Example of Love 149

Chickens in Church 151

Get Out Of Here! No Mas! . . 154

Obedience 101 157

Frank 160

Take My Heart Out
and Smash It 166

Gobsmacked 168

Lady at Publix 170

Glenses. 174

Who's Got Sense? 177

The Best People 180

Girl In A Blue-
Striped Sweater. 182

The Customs of Customs 184

Eating an Elephant. 199

Ten Penny Nail. 201

Tell Me More 204

The Mayor's Greedy Wife. . . . 206

More Shelving 211

Going to Jail. 213

$21.57 215

The Graduation Money 219

Stories of Giving. 222

Lunch at Wendy's. 226

Make More Pies 229

The Annual Report. 231

Extraordinary 238

Giving The Best Gift Ever . . . 240

What's Better? 243

Are You Comfortable Now? . . 245

Choosing The Right Power. . . 248

Humble Pie 251

The Man With
The Pizza Sign 255

Did I Cause That? 258

Moving 261

Stay With Me. 265

Plans I Have For You 267

My Hope 271

"I am sending you to them to open their eyes and turn them from darkness to light and from the power of Satan to God."

Chapter One

STRANGER IN A STRANGE LAND

I paused when I noticed a narrow beam of sunlight breaking through a crack in the unpainted concrete block wall. For a moment, I felt connected to it as we were both shattering a bit of the darkness that surrounded us. Outside just a few yards away, hundreds of half-naked children and shoeless adults were rummaging through one of Nicaragua's largest garbage dumps. A hundred shacks, made from cardboard, broken pallets, torn sheets of rusty tin, and moldy blankets, surrounded that field of garbage like a beat-up old frame around an ugly painting.

We had been seeing patients for hours in a small, dark, storage room positioned in the back of a pole barn church walled with cinder blocks. It was the best place around to host the eye clinic. Scores of people filled this building hoping we would be able to help them see.

Everyone on our team fought back fatigue as we realized how many patients still needed to be helped.

By the afternoon I was exhausted and bathed in sweat. The sun-scorched aluminum roof was cooking us like meat in a convection oven, and the unfelt breeze from a nearby fan only served to circulate the heat even more.

Every day we were there we served soup to hundreds of children for lunch. For many of them, this would be the only meal they would eat for the day. Some days there was no wood available for cooking the soup. The local women would improvise by burning plastic chairs. These chairs had been donated so that when this building was used for church the congregation wouldn't have to sit on the concrete floor. The poisonous fumes from those burning chairs added to the stench of rotten food, human waste, and dead animal carcasses coming from the garbage dump. The smells made me nauseated, and my eyes burned from the smoke.

"HOW IN THE WORLD DID I END UP HERE?" I PONDERED for a moment.

Slowly a smile formed on my face because I realized the answer to that question.

"To get here all I had to do was to give up everything … everything that I once thought was important, but really wasn't."

We were there to provide sight to the poor.

A LADY SAT IN FRONT OF ME ON ONE OF THOSE flimsy white plastic chairs. She was younger than me by almost twenty years, but she looked much older. Her clothes were worn and modest. She wore no makeup, and her hair was frizzy and unkempt. It felt like we came from different planets. As soon as I finished diagnosing her vision needs, I had an overwhelming desire to find out more about her.

She told me she was a believer, and that she loved Jesus. When those words reached my ears, all our differences dissolved. Instantly I felt deeply bonded to her. It was as if she was a long-lost sister of mine and somehow, we were separated when she was born. And now, all these years later, there she was right in front of me. Compassion filled me, I hugged her tightly and tears welled up in our eyes. I wanted to know all about her life and how it came about that she was living in a garbage dump.

She told me how Hurricane Mitch had hit Nicaragua. She and tens of thousands of others had lost their homes due to the heavy winds and flooding. The government had been overwhelmed trying to house so many displaced people. She and many other families were moved to the dump for temporary shelter. The government, however, severely lacking in resources, had left them there and forgotten all about them. It had been 18 years since they first arrived, and the people were still doing the best they could with what little they had. I listened as she continued with numerous stories of the hardships she had endured throughout her life and eventually my eyes filled with tears once again.

I walked with her to a nearby small storefront shack where I bought some snacks and drinks for her and her family. I gave her the rest of my money and prayed with her. Then I returned to the clinic. I did not want to let her go but had to get back to work. There were many still waiting for us to improve their eyesight.

I met a long-lost sister of mine that day. I was able to spend a few beautiful moments with her. Then I lost her again as she disappeared into the crowd on her way back home to one of those shacks. During our brief encounter, she had won over my heart. My hope, now, is that one day in Heaven we will be reunited and that there her hardships will be permanently removed.

Everybody has a story they need to tell, even those living in a garbage dump. I have one, too, and that is why I decided to write this book. I want my grandchildren to know their grandfather's stories.

Psalm 78:4 says we should, *"Tell the next generation the praiseworthy deeds of the Lord, his power, and the wonders he has done."*

Chapter Two
THE BEGINNING

At the age of 48, I was a suburban achiever, and everything in my life was proceeding as I planned. I had three wonderful children, a successful career, a sweet dog, and a beautiful wife, Jennifer. We lived in a pristine planned community thirty miles outside of Atlanta, Georgia, in the picture-perfect town of Peachtree City. Known by locals as "The Bubble," it is full of lush golf courses, crystalline pools, beautiful lakes, miles and miles of golf cart paths, flawlessly manicured yards, and unblemished tennis courts. Schools are highly rated, and crime is not even in the inhabitants' vocabulary. I was living life in "The Comfort Zone."

It's a beautiful place, but amidst the beauty, there lies a hidden danger. One does not often grow spiritually when surrounded by such comfort and abundance.

We regularly attended church on Sundays, as is the habit of most people in the South. Often, we attended various other church activities. Some years we hosted small group Bible studies, and much of our social life revolved around friends who did the same. Indeed, I was earning an *A* in what I called "Churchianity."

One summer, listening to our pastor speak, I was only paying half attention, as usual, but he said something that struck me. He used the word *legacy* in a sentence and my thoughts suddenly and unexpectedly began to focus only on what my legacy might be.

I suppose there comes a time in everyone's life when one reflects on the meaning of life and why we are here. This was my time for that. I knew what my plans were for my life. I was going to open yet another optical business and get it running successfully. Then we would have enough income to retire early and move to Aruba. There we would indulge ourselves by playing golf every day, and, afterward, relax on the beach while sipping umbrella drinks. In that paradise, we would perfect our tans, and in the evenings, we'd stroll down the beach to enjoy dinners at beautiful oceanfront restaurants.

That was my plan. My legacy would be to leave behind a family that was financially secure so that my offspring would be able to enjoy whatever dreams they desired. For a moment, however, I began to wonder if there may be something more to life than a well-diversified portfolio and my plans for a future hedonistic lifestyle.

"WHAT COULD I ACCOMPLISH TO LEAVE THIS WORLD a better place?"

After pondering this for a while, I said a prayer, asking God (almost rhetorically) "What is my legacy going to be?"

I HAVE HEARD IT SAID THAT YOU ARE RARELY PRE-pared for the moment that changes your life. Just a few seconds can change everything. It could be a knock on the door from the police saying there's been an accident or a call from the doctor confirming you have cancer. Maybe your employer notifies you that the company you have dedicated yourself to for decades is downsizing and you're no longer needed.

Well, little did I realize that this was the moment that would begin to change my life. Immediately after asking God what my legacy would be, I heard a voice. This voice spoke ten simple words that dramatically reshaped my life.

"You're going to make eyeglasses for the world's poorest people," said the voice.

I turned around to see if someone behind me was playing some sort of a joke, but there was no one there. I was stunned. I had never had audible hallucinations in my life, and I knew that I did not have schizophrenia. I am positive, though, that I heard a voice that morning.

Never in my life had I considered making eyeglasses for poor people. Early in my career, I decided I would cater to wealthy people. You could earn a lot more money that way. Why would I spend all my time selling eyeglasses for $49 when people with resources would buy nice pairs for $800?

After hearing this voice out of nowhere, I turned to my wife and whispered, "I'm going to make eyeglasses for the world's poorest people."

"That's nice, Dear, now be quiet and listen to the sermon," she said.

However, for the rest of the sermon, all I could hear was, "Blah, blah, blah." Something had just happened to me that I could not explain.

When we arrived home, my wife and I talked more about it. I was fired up and excited. I did a Google search to find out how many poor people needed eyeglasses. The World Health Organization estimated that 517 million poor people needed glasses. The Oxford Medical College estimated that over a billion people in the world would never obtain the eyeglasses they needed. Other estimates even declared that over two billion people could never afford eye care!

Almost immediately, I concluded there were far too many people who needed help and it would be pointless to take on a project of that enormity. It was an unfortunate dilemma that had no answer. My enthusiasm and joy dissipated quickly. I was rather disappointed with how easily I could dismiss the incredible moment I had with God just hours before.

Chapter Three
THANKS, JENN!

One evening, three weeks after I heard the voice in church, my wife Jenn said she urgently needed to talk with me.

"What's up, Babe?" I asked her.

"Well, today I googled "medical mission organizations" and I emailed several of them, offering that you are willing to make their eyeglasses for free."

"Why did you do that?" I snapped back at her. "Do you know how much that will cost us?"

Her generosity with our funds and my time upset me. I quickly calculated the cost in my head and immediately concluded it would certainly interfere with any plans to retire early. This was not part of my life's plan. Aruba was still calling me.

Despite my frustration, she responded softly in the kindest, most loving way.

"I did it because when God tells you to do something, you should do it."

Those words pierced my heart. I knew she was right. I said nothing and stared at the floor.

She had done it and there was not much I could do about it now. I kept thinking that when you offer to do something for free that millions of people will respond to you. I was secretly hoping that G-mail would shut down my account due to an overflow of responses. But an unusual thing happened. No one responded to her offers! I was so relieved. I had dodged a bullet!

A few weeks later, however, we did get one emailed response. It was from an American eye doctor named Valerie Colby. She was an optometrist, serving in Honduras as a missionary, running a small eye clinic.

"Yes, we would love your help!" she wrote. "The people I serve here are extremely poor; they cannot afford eyeglasses."

Her response created a huge dilemma for me. I had what I believed to be a clear calling from God as to what He wanted me to do and now I had a real live person who was expecting a response from me. The only problem was, that I didn't want to do it. Not one bit. It would cost me a lot of extra time and money and it just made no sense to me at all.

This dilemma caused the first of many nights of interrupted sleep for me. For Christians, sometimes the biggest battle in life is the one that goes on in our hearts and minds. I was unable to stop thinking about it. I woke up often, tossing and turning with thoughts of making glasses for the poor. I couldn't turn it off. I secretly hoped that it would all go away, but it did not. No matter how hard I tried, I couldn't justify doing this work for free. Heck, I couldn't even justify doing it even at wholesale costs.

I owned an optical lab inside of a highly successful large eye practice. I was well compensated for my efforts. I have made tens of thousands of pairs of eyeglasses over the years. The work and the demands of patients were steadily beginning to wear on me. I didn't have even the slightest desire to edge more lenses and not get paid for it. The entire concept seemed utterly absurd.

A couple of weeks had passed, and I was once again tossing and turning in bed. Around 3 a.m. the voice returned and was whispering to me. I knew somehow, I was supposed to read a verse in the Bible: Matthew 6:22-23. I did not hear it audibly, but it just played in my head over and over: Matthew 6:22-23, Matthew 6:22-23, Matthew 6:22-23...

I went to my library and pulled one of my many seldom-read Bibles off the shelf. This is what I read: Matthew 6:22-23:

"The eye is the lamp of the body. If your eye is healthy, then your whole body will be full of light, but if your eye is bad, your whole body will be full of darkness. If the light that is within you is in darkness, then how terrible is that darkness!"

When Jesus spoke those words thousands of years ago, he was referring to the eye in a spiritual context, but the moment I read it, I realized for me it also applied to the physical. I knew if our physical eyes didn't work, we would be in darkness and that is a terrible thing indeed. At that moment, it dawned on me that there are billions of people drowning in a sea of darkness (metaphorically speaking) and I owned a lifeboat with the supplies needed to help them. How could I live with myself if I wouldn't even throw them a life preserver?

At that moment everything became crystal clear. The next piece of my life was right in front of me. This realization started the first of many spiritual changes that were to occur inside of me over the next several years. Slowly I began to entertain the thought that I would somehow attempt to help the poor to see. Well, at least a few of them.

The next day I emailed Dr. Valerie Colby. (Remember that name for a few minutes, Dr. Valerie Colby) I told her I would be willing to send optical supplies to her and I asked for her address. The reply was unexpected.

"Our address is the blue building with two bushes and a white sign with red letters on it near Armando's bus stop…there are no addresses where we work, '' she wrote.

A short time later I obtained her phone number and called her.

"How can I send supplies to you? Do you have mail?"

"No," she replied.

"Do you have FedEx?"

"Nope."

"How about UPS or DHL?"

"No," she again replied.

"Well, how am I going to get supplies to you?" I asked.

"I don't know."

And that's how the call ended.

Chapter Four

THE CONVENTION

After that phone call, I was perplexed as to why a part of me felt so deeply convinced that God wanted me to help Dr. Valerie when there was no apparent way to send her supplies. Then a thought came to me, and I suddenly believed I understood what God was up to.

I brilliantly concluded that all of this was an "Abraham and Isaac moment" and I was just being tested.

For those of you unfamiliar with that biblical story, there was a man named Abraham, and one day instead of the usually required sacrifice, the Lord asked him to sacrifice his son instead. Abraham trusted God enough to do that and just as Abraham was getting ready to plunge a knife into his son an angel stopped him and told him he was just being tested. God was testing Abraham to see if he would obey Him no matter what He asked him to do.

I rationalized that this was what was happening to me. Since getting eye-glasses to Honduras seemed to be an impossibility, God must have been just testing me to see if I would be willing to do something I didn't want to do. Yes, that is all it was, a test! And since I was willing to do it, I thought that I had passed the test with flying colors.

"Go ahead and send me the T-shirt, God!"

I convinced myself that I never had to follow through on making free eyeglasses for the poor. I only needed to agree to do it. Now I could finally just forget about this whole crazy idea.

And that's exactly what I did. I no longer thought about it and I was once again able to sleep peacefully through the night. I mentally gave myself a big pat on the back for being willing to do it. Falsely I convinced myself that I had passed the Lord's testing.

A few more weeks went by, and I once again had another annoying moment happen at church. During the time for announcements, the pastor mentioned that The National Missionary Convention for Christian Churches was being held in Atlanta, Georgia, that year. He said it was starting on Thursday and going through Sunday of the upcoming week.

"If any of you are interested in missions, you should attend, " He said. I winced.

At that time in my life, I had absolutely no interest at all in missions. I didn't personally know any missionaries, not even one. I knew what they did, and I believed they were good people who devoted their lives to doing good things, but I had no personal desire to do that. After all, it didn't pay well.

Throughout the week God was encouraging me to attend this conference. I was beginning to think I should just quit going to church altogether if stuff like this was going to keep happening.

"I'm never going to go to that convention! Never ever never!" I told myself over and over.

Immediately the sleepless nights returned.

Wednesday evening, I began to make up an excuse as to why I could not attend on Thursday. I told myself that I had patients coming in that would only want to see me and that I had to be at the office for them. So, I didn't go.

And at this point in my life, things were going so well that I frequently played golf on Friday at noon. There was no way I was giving up a golf day to go to a stupid missionary conference. So, as usual, I played golf instead.

That night I became an insomniac once again. Something inside of my head kept telling me that I was supposed to go to the convention. No more voices; however, the mental nudging was relentless. I couldn't take it any longer.

I gave in and early Saturday morning I woke up my wife and told her that I had to go to that stupid missionary convention. Immediately she jumped out of bed and grabbed my coat and keys.

"Go! Go, find out what God has planned for you!"

Then, she went back to bed. I had hoped she would at least go with me.

During the 45-minute drive to Atlanta, I complained the entire way. I imagined that there would be around fifty missionaries there standing around soliciting donations. I was sure there would be a bunch of overweight men wearing black suits with white shirts and cheap ties and the women would be sporting bouffant hairdos and wearing lots of heavy makeup.

Thoughts and questions began to flood my head. How would I know which one to talk to? What would I do if the missionaries formed a circle surrounding me, holding my hands and forcing me to sing "Kumbaya" with them?

I think you get the gist. I didn't want to go and several times I thought about turning around and going back home.

When I finally arrived, I was surprised to discover that there were not just fifty people there. There were more than seven thousand people and several hundred missionary groups with display booths. I thought to myself that this was just like the eye conventions that I attend in Las Vegas and New York City. I had no idea that missionaries held these types of conventions. I didn't know, in this mob of seven thousand, who I was supposed to see.

I paused in the lobby and somehow remembered a story from the Bible from when I was a child. There was a man named Gideon who owned a fleece. He thought that God wanted him to do something, but he wasn't 100 percent sure if that thought was from God or not so he proposed a test. He told God that when he left his fleece outside at night and checked in the morning if his fleece was wet and everyone else's fleece was dry, he would know the command was from God. The next morning it was wet and everyone else had dry ones. That still didn't convince Gideon, so he told God to do the opposite the next night and that also happened. Gideon still wasn't convinced. So again, he asked God to do it a third time and God did. Finally, Gideon was convinced that it was indeed God asking him to do something.

I decided I would devise my own modern-day version of Gideon's fleece test. I told God that I would walk all around the exhibit hall and read about each group's endeavors. I stipulated I wasn't going to talk to anyone, however, if I thought their mission possibly had something to do with getting eyeglasses to poor people, I would write their names down on a piece of paper. Then after I wandered around the entire exhibit hall, I would find myself a quiet corner, pull out the paper, and question God.

"Which of these groups should I talk to? If you will illuminate their name on the paper, I'll go talk with them. If you do that, I'll know this whole plan about getting eyeglasses for the poor is from you. "

Sounded like a good plan to me!

So that's what I did. For four hours and ten minutes I meandered around the exhibit hall and avoided eye contact with anyone. When I was in the last row, a friendly missionary lady stepped up to me.

"Hi, what are you doing here?

"I have no idea what I'm doing here."

That reply caused her to chuckle.

"I think I'm supposed to help poor people get eyeglasses, but I have no idea who I'm supposed to see here," I said with frustration.

"I know EXACTLY who you are supposed to see!"

That caught me off guard and it piqued my curiosity.

"There's a group here called F.A.M.E. It's an acronym for Fellowship for the Advancement of Medical Evangelists and you are supposed to see them," she explained.

Then I pulled the list out of my pocket. I held it up to her. After over four hours of walking around, I had written only one name on that paper and it was "F.A.M.E" ... and the letters were glowing! (No, not really, but that would have been amazing!)

As I showed her their name on my paper, she pointed down the exhibit hall.

"They are about twenty rows over and about halfway towards the back wall. I returned to the F.A.M.E booth and this time I spoke with the man who represented that group.

"May I help you?"

"I believe I am supposed to make eyeglasses for poor people, but I don't know who to help."

"I know EXACTLY who you are supposed to help," he said matter-of-factly.

That was the second time I had heard those words in the past three minutes.

"Where were you guys four hours ago?" I thought to myself.

Next, he took his finger and pointed it against my chest.

"You are supposed to help ... Dr. Valerie Colby in Honduras."

Out of all the millions of missionaries in the world, he had just named the only one who had ever contacted me!

I was shocked and unable to talk for about two minutes. Anyone who knows me would find that to be unbelievable.

Up to this point in my life, other than my wife, I had told no one about my contact with Dr. Colby. Nobody ever knew that she replied to me or that we had ever conversed with one another. When I finally could speak, I told him that I had previously spoken with her and that we did not know how I could get supplies to her mission in Honduras. He then informed me that his mission group takes teams of medical people down to her mission base a couple of times every year. He finished by saying if I sent eye supplies to their headquarters in Indianapolis, Indiana, they would be happy to hand deliver the supplies directly to her.

I picked up his business card and walked away wondering what had just happened. I left the convention and walked out of the building and looked up to the sky and said, "You really want me to do this, don't you!"

I didn't know it then, but that was the moment that God's Eyes ministry was born.

Chapter Five
TAKING BABY STEPS

One day a few weeks after the missionary convention in Atlanta, I decided to take a small step toward helping the poor to see. I told my wife I was going to start a nonprofit corporation. I mentioned that I was always fond of the name "Kaiz Eyes," named after myself, of course, but she replied that she thought it should be called "God's Eyes."

When she said that, something clicked inside of me, and I knew she was right. Amazingly, it took all of five seconds to decide on the name.

A friend helped us with some of the initial paperwork. Next, the wife of one of my patients, who owned a law firm, notified me that her husband's business partner was willing to incorporate us. He did all the paperwork for us to obtain our nonprofit status pro bono.

Hmmm, I began to think that maybe God was in this somehow. But then again, maybe some people just have good hearts, and they do nice things. I wasn't sure which.

I knew nothing about running a not-for-profit corporation. I only knew how to make money and keep it, not how to give it away. And how would I ever give money away if we never raised money in the first place? I knew we wouldn't be selling anything.

Then it hit me. I should do what I thought everyone else did, what every church and every group and every person I ever knew who went into missions did, and that was to ask people for money. Yeah, that's what we would do. We would write letters to everyone we knew requesting donations. I had received so many of those letters in my life that I couldn't even begin to count them all. Like them, I would notify everyone of the amazing works we planned on undertaking.

Certainly, we could convince people to donate. Perhaps I should say "persuade" people … it sounds much less manipulative. I was well known in my town. After working for twenty years at the largest and arguably the best eye care practice around, I had come to know thousands of patients over time, many of whom were extremely wealthy. Jenn and I even had family members, on both sides, who were wealthy. Certainly, they would all contribute to our new, worthy cause.

During this time, however, two things occurred. First, I arbitrarily obtained a book titled *The Biography of George Muller* and read it. I learned that George was a pastor in England in the 1800s and he ran orphanages without ever asking men for money. He learned to trust only in God, and, through prayer alone, all the needs of his ministry were met. It was a fascinating read, and I wondered how and why so many ministries had changed from that model of trusting only in God, to today's model of asking people for everything.

Second, during this time, my Bible reading increased from once in a blue moon to much more frequently. One day I happened to read the sixth chapter of the Gospel of John. It records the story about the feeding of the five thousand.

If you're unfamiliar with that story, here's a summary: Jesus and his disciples were up on a mountain and a huge crowd of people gathered to listen to Jesus. He then tested the disciples.

"Where will we buy food for these people to eat?" he said.

"Even two hundred days' wages wouldn't be enough to feed everyone."

That reply came from a disciple named Philip. I imagine he must have been one of those practical math major types and I instantly became a fan of his.

Here's what I think Philip meant:

Who cares where we could get food! Even if there was a place that could make thousands of meals nearby, it would be impossible for us to pay for the food. We don't have anywhere close to enough money.

"What do you have?" the Lord asked them.

"A small boy has given us five loaves of bread and two fishes."

Then Jesus asked for and was given those resources and He began to distribute them. Somehow, they multiplied until five thousand men had eaten all that they could. In addition to those men, there may have been thousands of women and children there who were fed as well. Afterward, Jesus told the disciples to pick up all the leftover food.

They gathered up so much that twelve large baskets were filled with leftovers.

THERE ARE MANY SIMILARITIES BETWEEN THAT STORY and what was taking place in my life. In the bible story, the disciples have a problem: How are they going to feed so many people? In my world, I had a problem as well: How was I going to buy eyeglasses for so many people?

In the bible story Jesus asks, "What resources do you have to offer towards solving this problem," and they answer, "Five loaves of bread and two fishes."

At that time Jesus was asking me the same question, "What do you have?"

"A savings account and some money set aside for retirement," I cautiously replied.

In the story, the disciples gladly handed over their resources, and the Lord used what the disciples offered to accomplish something impossible. Thousands of people were fed despite an extreme lack of provisions.

IN MY LIFE, THE LORD SIMPLY ASKED ME TO DO THE same, to give Him what I had.

What I had dreaded was coming true. God expected me to have some financial skin in this game. That's when I "went Moses" on him. Read Exodus chapter 4 if you don't know what I mean!

In my head, I had the following thoughts: You've got the wrong guy! Everything I have is MINE! It's my money. I earned it. I've worked long and hard for it! That money is for me and my family to enjoy. This whole thing about giving glasses to the poor has been fun while it lasted, but if you think I'm going to pay for it, you must be mistaken!

And just like Moses, I pleaded with God to find someone else for the job. But the Lord persisted and quietly whispered to me again:

"Just give me what you have."

ONCE AGAIN, THE SLEEPLESS NIGHTS RETURNED. I found myself trying to negotiate with God. Reluctantly I offered to tithe on my gross income, not my net income, and again I heard Him reply softly:

"Just give me what you have."

After a short time went by, I generously upped my offer to twenty percent.

"Just give me what you have," He said. More weeks of restless sleep went by, and I increased my offer to 30 percent. The same reply came back in a kind of gentle nudging, encouraging me to give what I had. I struggled deeply with this. Why should I give up my money?

"Tell other people to give money, in fact, PLEASE ask someone else to do this whole thing," I told God. "I'm willing to help but just let me keep what's mine."

Weeks passed by and sometimes I would briefly fall asleep during the day at my lab from sleep deprivation. Other nights, I tossed and turned while questioning why I was being picked on. All the time I was hoping He would ask someone else to do this.

My lack of sleep must have been fogging my mind because eventually, I raised my offer to 40 percent. Each time I heard the same response:

"Bryan, just give me what you have."

ONE NIGHT AMIDST THE STRUGGLE, GOD WHISPERED to me again:

"Bryan, why is this so hard for you? You tell everyone at church that all you have is from me!"

I had no response. After pondering for several minutes, I finally shamefully confessed:

"I know I say that but, I just realized I don't mean it. I've heard other people say it at church and it sounds profoundly spiritual that I've added it to my "Churchianity" vocabulary. I confessed that I only said it because it sounds like something a good Christian should say.

It made me realize that it's so much easier to "talk the talk," than it is to "walk the walk." I felt ashamed of myself. It was like I'd been cheating on a test, and I just got caught. In desperation a few nights later I told God that I was submitting my final offer:

"This is all I have in me, Lord. It's the best I can do. I will give you 50 percent of what I have now, and I will give you the other 50 percent when I die. I will leave everything I have to the church. My kids can fend for themselves. Fifty percent now and 50 percent later when I die, adds up to 100 percent. Take it or leave it."

I desperately hoped the Lord would accept my offer.

He responded to me with a question:

"How many people did the first five loaves and two fish feed?" I had never thought of that before.

"Hmmm, I don't know, Lord, maybe five or ten people depending on the size of the fish."

What Father was teaching me was that the supplies of the disciples ran out rather quickly. Five loaves of bread and two fish don't feed a lot of people. The miracle of multiplication, however, happened only after the resources of those asked to give, ran out. Not before.

Father certainly didn't need any of my resources, but I would have to exhaust what I had before I could see Him work.

I suddenly realized if the disciples had made the offer I did, to give 50 percent ... two-and-a-half bread loaves and one fish ... that day, do you know what would have happened? I believe that five thousand men would not have been fed. And what if they would have matched my offer, to wait until they died to donate the other half of what they had. By then the bread would have molded, and the fish would have rotted.

You see, their supplies had value that day. The people there were hungry and needed to be fed that day, not years later. I concluded the same applied to people who needed vision correction.

Something inside of me broke that night as I realized how my greed might be the reason that someone wouldn't get to see clearly. My disobedience had consequences for other people. If I only offered half of my resources, how many people would have to live decades with uncorrected sight before the rest of my money might buy them glasses? What if they died before me and I could have given them the ability to see clearly and I didn't? Could it be true that God would pour out more if I were to go in all the way? What if my selfishness was preventing a miracle? Could He and would He multiply my resources to help people? I knew what I needed to do.

My heart broke open that night and my worldview began to expand. Perhaps a child in the Philippines, an old man in India, or a woman in Africa would be able to see if I was willing to release the hold on my finances.

That night I told God if He would help me, I would go all in, financially speaking, if he kept prospering me. At the same time, I was hoping my inner reluctance would not stop me from keeping that promise.

I decided that God's Eyes should follow the example set by George Muller. I wouldn't write letters to people. I would use my resources and with what little faith I had, I would try to muster up enough courage to be obedient and trust that God would eventually show up.

Jenn and I scaled down our lifestyle. No more country club membership, no more golf, swimming pools, or tennis, no more expensive vacations and we canceled the gym memberships as well. We made cutbacks wherever we could.

It was hard, though, not to worry as I watched our resources begin to dwindle.

Chapter Six
MEETING VALERIE

Shortly after I attended the Atlanta missionary convention, I started sending eye care supplies to Dr. Valerie Colby through F.A.M.E. 's headquarters in Indiana. She started emailing me patients' prescription orders and I filled them. Every month this went on. I believe the first order I sent back was three pairs of glasses.

Over the next few months, we found an additional way to get supplies down to her. A captain from American Airlines flew to Honduras regularly and she would hide our eye supplies in suitcases full of donated used old clothing. That way everything went through customs without being stolen as sometimes happens. This plan worked well and the size of the orders increased.

A few months later a doctor from Haiti somehow heard about me. She called me and asked if I would start filling her orders.

I told her "Yes," but said, "Please go easy on me as this is all on my nickel."

Her orders were much larger than Dr. Colby's and soon I was making many pairs of new prescription eyeglasses every month for them. Both would usually send me the more difficult and costly prescriptions to make. Some of those extremely high-powered lenses ran over $150 a pair, wholesale, just for the material.

Over the next few months, uneasy feelings began to creep in and I became a bit concerned about the time and expense that it was costing me. I knew

I had agreed to help, but it was quickly becoming more than I anticipated. I knew that what I was doing was the right thing to do and the good thing to do and that it even gave me some sense of pride. Still, on the inside, I was complaining to myself about the costs and some days I even resented that I had said "yes." Begrudgingly, I continued sending supplies.

After fourteen months of filling the prescription orders, one of my church's assistant pastors, who also happened to be a physician, asked me if I would like to go to Honduras and meet Dr. Valerie Colby. I quickly said yes. I wanted to check out who it was I was sending so many supplies to. I thought that if I met her and saw what she was doing, maybe it would help me feel better about the expenses I was incurring. Our church partnered up with F.A.M.E and together they planned a trip for a group of about a dozen people to visit Honduras on a medical trip.

Two months later I loaded up several suitcases full of frames and hundreds of lens blanks that are used to make prescription eyeglasses. They would be donated to Valerie's eye clinic. I also brought the latest orders of eyeglasses that she had requested.

I had never been to a third-world country before and the stories I began to hear of how dangerous it was in Honduras began to freak me out a little. Due to this, I wasn't as excited as I thought I would be by the time we left.

We flew to Honduras through Miami and things started with a bang … literally. Just as our jet's wheels left the tarmac in Miami, one of its engines exploded and the pilot immediately had to abort and put the plane back down. We hit the runway hard, and the pilot slammed on the brakes.

"This must be some kind of an omen!" I thought.

After a short time on the runway, we returned to the gate and de-boarded. They said we would all have to wait several hours until another plane became available. It was the excuse I was looking for. I thought it must be a sign from God that we weren't supposed to go, and I was ready to fly back to Atlanta.

"Surely everyone else in the group must be thinking the same thing," I thought.

But nobody else verbalized any such thoughts, so I sucked it up and kept it to myself.

SEVERAL HOURS LATER WE ARRIVED IN HONDURAS and were picked up in trucks, but some of us had to stand in the truck beds with all the luggage.

"This is ridiculous!" I grumbled to myself, "Why didn't they just bring enough vehicles for us all to sit inside. Are they trying to kill us all?"

I would find out quickly that this is quite the norm for travel in Honduras. We drove through Tegucigalpa and then up into the mountains zig-zagging the switchbacks on what they refer to as roads. I discovered why there were no addresses there. The entire sides of many of the mountains were littered with shacks.

For the first time in my life, I was immersed in third-world poverty.

FINALLY, THERE IT WAS! VALERIE'S "ADDRESS." THE large blue building with two bushes and a white sign with red letters on it near a bus stop. This was the compound where we would be living for the next seven nights. We unloaded all our supplies and later we gathered for dinner in the living room at the compound. At last, I was face to face with Valerie.

There's something special about missionaries who live in third-world countries. It is disarming. Valerie is one of those unique people who are so full of love and joy that everyone who meets her instantly loves her, and so did I.

After dinner, we had a group meeting where we discussed the agenda for the week and learned the rules for the compound. Some of the rules seemed quite strange to me. We could not flush toilet paper down the bowl. We had to throw it into a wastebasket next to the toilet. We weren't supposed to flush the toilet at all if all we did was pee. We were to let it linger until someone finally had a bowel movement, and then it could be flushed. The explanation had something to do with the inadequate septic system and the size of the sewer lines. I think you can well imagine what bathrooms smell like in Honduras.

Valerie had a little jingle to make this all sound better: "If it's brown, flush it down, but if it's yellow, let it mellow."

To a little ol' suburban boy with no camping experience, this seemed quite disturbing.

Things quickly got worse. After the meeting, she informed us that the girls would sleep in the bunk beds in the bedrooms of the upstairs apartment. When I inquired where the men were going to sleep, she announced that the guys would stay in the unfinished basement of the garage.

I believed she must have been joking so I said, "No seriously, where are we staying?" She repeated herself, "The basement of the garage."

They took us across the parking lot to the garage and told us not to leave the compound at night. That was fine with me but I asked her, ``What would happen if we did leave?" and she said, "Well if you do, you'll meet Jesus."

Great, so now we were going to die if we stepped outside the compound … good to know! I was sure that information would help me sleep better that night.

In the basement, there were several mattresses. Some were on frames, but most were just set on the cement floor. I saw a three-inch-long black scorpion crawling into a book on one of my friends' chosen beds. Trevor, who is Valerie's husband, told us not to worry about the scorpions.

"You won't die from their stings," he said, "it only feels like a bee sting."

It was so comforting to learn that once we were locked in the basement I no longer had to fear death, instead, I would only get stung by scorpions.

He also informed us that the two showers were heated by "widow-makers." Widow-makers are small heaters that are attached to the showerhead. If you adjust the water flow so that it trickles out slowly, the water becomes a little bit warmer before it hits your body. I must emphasize "a little bit warmer." He also said that we should not raise our hands above our heads.

"If you have wet hands and accidentally touch the wires on the shower head heater, it will electrocute you."

I've always been somewhat of a hotel snob. I always wanted to stay at the finest accommodations I could afford while on trips. I had never stayed at a

Motel 6 in my life. This was "Motel Minus 6!" I can just hear their slogan now: "We'd leave a light on for you ... if we had a light."

For the following five or six days, we held medical and eye clinics in different villages within a driving radius of a couple of hours. I was so excited. For the first time in my life, I was helping the poor to see. Not poor as defined in America as "the poverty level," but I mean extremely poor. Poor as in living in disgusting shacks with no food, water, or electricity. The villages we worked in were eye-opening... no pun intended. This introduction to real poverty would have a permanent effect on me.

One day we worked in a little village called Via de San Francisco. Valerie told me that one of the pairs of prescription eyeglasses I had made back in the States was for a seven-year-old girl, Lissette. She was from that village and had been born into a family who knew all too well what the phrase, life *is not fair, was* all about.

My hands were shaking as I dispensed the eyeglasses to Lissette. Of all of the eyeglasses I had made during the previous fourteen months for Valerie, this was the first one I delivered to its intended recipient.

The realization that the glasses I had been making were bringing sight to real people was overwhelming. I was overjoyed and stood in awe as Lissette experienced clear vision for the first time in her life. My eyes welled up with tears. She hugged me, smiled ever so graciously, and left. I watched her as she walked away showing off her new glasses to the other kids in the village. It was one of those moments in my life that I will never forget. Instantly I was hooked. I began to think this is what I was created to do.

Cell phones were just becoming popular back then. Only a few would work in foreign countries; mine did not. Carolyn, one of my friends on the trip, had a satellite phone that could call back home to the States. One night, about five days into the trip, I borrowed it to call my wife. She asked me how the trip was.

"It is every word and its opposite," I said. "It is beautiful, and it is ugly. It is wonderful and it is horrible. It is delightful, and it is depressing. It is pure joy, and it is heart-wrenching."

I've now since been on nearly one hundred such trips and I've yet to describe what it's like to be on a mission trip any better than that.

On the last day we held the clinics, we drove to the furthest location from the compound. It took us a few hours to get there. On the way, I realized how incredibly comfortable I had become as I stood up in a truck bed while the driver played "chicken" with the oncoming traffic.

Strangely, it was exhilarating to be a part of that game while the wind blew in my face. The cool breeze also offered comfort from the oppressive heat. Once the paved highway ended, the roads to this village became like minefields. They had ruts in the dirt and mud deep enough to tip over a car. Some of the potholes were filled with water deep enough to bathe in. Ok, perhaps that's a slight exaggeration, but the last two miles of traveling up the final steep hill took us over an hour. After we arrived, we had to transport all the medical supplies across a rope suspension bridge with wooden steps. It dangled, precariously, fifty feet above a large, rapidly moving river.

The day before I had depleted all the eye supplies I had brought with me on the trip, so instead of dispensing new eyeglasses, I helped the pharmacy team. We counted and packaged pills to fill the prescriptions the medical doctors were writing. I spent an entire day distributing medications. As I handed out each prescription, I decided to practice my Spanish. That was a mistake!

I thought I said "God bless you" to everyone after handing their medicine to them when in fact, I had requested that they bless me. They must have thought I was full of myself.

During the morning at the clinic, one of our team members came up to me and handed me an eyeglass prescription. A patient had just arrived and had given it to her in hopes of procuring a pair of eyeglasses. I was puzzled as to where he could have possibly acquired a written prescription in such an isolated location, but somehow, he did. The lady who handed me the prescription asked me what she should say to him, and I told her that I would speak with him directly.

I grabbed a translator and headed over to the man. On the walk over I remember how badly I felt because I was about to tell him that I couldn't help him. I hadn't come three thousand miles to tell people I couldn't fix their sight when helping people see was the exact reason I was on this trip. My heart ached as I approached him.

He was a small frail man with dark wrinkled skin wearing dirty clothes. He was counting on me. I saw the sad look in his eyes. I was his hope. I didn't want to look directly into his eyes. I didn't want to see the disappointment on his face when I told him the bad news that we were out of prescription glasses.

As I stood in front of him, I looked down at the numbers on his prescription, and then I realized something amazing. His prescription for eyeglasses matched mine exactly! Number for number everything was the same!

I was so happy I abruptly took off my glasses and placed them on his face. He lit up and smiled from ear to ear as he looked around and saw everything in focus. I was full of joy and amazement that God had provided him with a pair of eyeglasses even after our supplies were exhausted.

I had just learned an important lesson that morning. God can make a way where there's no way. He can supply when there are no supplies!

I flew back to Atlanta the next day. It took only half a day after a few hours of layover in Miami. I told my wife all about the trip. At home, I flushed extra toilet paper down the drain just because I could. I even enjoyed dancing with my hands above my head when I took a hot water shower. I no longer needed to worry about being electrocuted.

I was only a few hours by plane from Honduras, but the differences made it seem like it was a universe away.

I was eager to tell others about my trip. I was shocked, however, when no one cared to hear about it. Only a few friends even bothered to ask me how the trip was and after I said, "Amazing" they simply replied, "That's great," and began to talk about something else.

The poverty in Honduras permanently affected my heart. So did Valerie and her family's effortless love. There was something taking place inside of me. My inner apathy was beginning to change to empathy.

Over the next couple of weeks, I found myself slowly returning to my previous way of life, but with two exceptions. I began to pray a bit more and I started reading my Bible even more often.

One night I came upon the book of Acts, chapter 26, the second part of verse 17, and the first part of verse 18:

"I am sending you to them to open their eyes and turn them from darkness to light and from the power of Satan to God."

That verse blew me away and it hit me hard. It was as if God had written it specifically for me.

"I am sending you, Bryan Kaiser, to open their eyes."

I knew at that instant not only was I to send supplies to the poor but that Father's plan involved sending me to them. I was to go to them and open their eyes no matter where they lived. I would also have to learn to become evangelistic, then I could help open their spiritual eyes and help turn them from Satan to God.

Every day I grew more dissatisfied with my career situation, and I felt a constant tugging to take a greater leap of faith. But how could I ever do that?

Chapter Seven
MUD COOKIES AND OTHER "DELIGHTS"

A few months after my trip to Honduras, the man I had met at the missionary conference, who had told me about helping Dr. Valerie Colby called me one day. He asked if I would accompany him as he traveled around Haiti on a ten-day trip to visit some of the medical ministries F.A.M.E. supported. He thought it would be good to introduce me to them, and perhaps God would reveal some kind of opportunity for me to partner with more groups in Haiti and supply them with eyeglasses. I would also get to meet the new eye doctor who took over for the doctor I had been sending supplies to. I had a strong conviction that this was a trip I was supposed to go on.

We flew with a couple of other men and arrived in Haiti late in the evening. Haiti is quite a strange place if you're used to comforts in the States. Most of the electricity is shut down at night. If a location had lights on, it was only because they had a generator. Driving through the dark streets of Port-au-Prince at night was an unsettling experience. The whole area had been dipped headfirst into a bucket of blackness. Eerie illumination came from fires lit on the sides of roads. The flickering infernos hauntingly revealed the horrific conditions Haitians were forced to survive in. It was like an end-of-the-world post-apocalyptic scene.

We arrived at a guest house (Haiti's equivalent of a motel). I was shaken from everything I'd seen on the drive there. There you did not get a room to yourself, you simply rented a bed in a room full of strangers, and everyone on that floor shared the same bathroom located down the hall. In our room, there were eight beds. Several Haitian strangers slept there with us. They were the loudest snorers I had ever heard. Being a novice at all this missionary travel, I didn't pack earplugs or bring sleeping pills with me. I lay awake all night listening to the deafening rumbles from them.

The next day we began a seven-hour journey to the north coast of Haiti. We arrived at a small local airport. Undoubtedly, I missed the memo that said to bring snacks and something to drink with you. They would have come in handy because there was nothing to eat or drink at this small local airport. At this small regional airfield you could wait for hours, or even days, before your flight would leave.

There was only one plane flying to where we were going, Port-de-Paix. Even though there were scheduled times for the planes to fly, they just departed whenever they decided to go. There was no air conditioning in the terminal. Due to the extreme heat in Haiti, to say I was uncomfortable was an understatement. I hadn't thought of all these things ahead of time or I would have brought snacks, water, and a fan! Naively, I thought it would be similar to flying to an isolated location in a smaller state in the U.S. Boy, was I ever wrong!

Eventually, a few hours behind schedule, we boarded an ancient single-engine airplane that sat nineteen people if the luggage didn't weigh too much. It looked like an old plane salvaged from a junkyard. I think the Wright brothers had scrapped it. It, too, had no air conditioning. The flight was deafening and sweltering. Only the pilot had a small window for air and it never made it to the rest of the plane.

Who doesn't have air conditioning nowadays for Pete's sake, I thought. Over the next several years of travel, I would learn that the answer to that question is, "most people in the world."

However, once I was in the air high above Haiti, the views of the mountains and the ocean were beautiful, that is, until we touched down and were once again neck-deep in poverty. The runway we landed on was also used as a road by the locals. When they saw the plane coming in for a landing, they calmly sauntered off to the side of the runway.

The trip was uncomfortable in almost every way and it was miserably hot! Bugs and mosquitoes were plentiful. There was so much poverty and need. It could be overwhelming for all but well-seasoned travelers.

On the second day, we arrived at a small medical mission base where they cared for hundreds of desperately sick and needy people. The missionaries and volunteers at the base were the best people in the world. They too had also learned to pour out love easily and abundantly.

As a "newbie" to the mission field, everything I saw and experienced was overwhelming. A lady died that day giving birth and the mission base gained yet another addition to their already overcrowded baby orphanage. This base had the only delivery room in the northwest corner of Haiti. It consisted of a mattress on top of a small desk.

This base did so much with so little. One of the nurses there told me that a man had arrived at the compound one day holding his intestines in his arms. He had been attacked with a machete and she wondered how she was ever going to be able to help him with such limited supplies. She told me she pushed his intestines back into his torso, sewed him up, and gave him Tylenol for pain and he left. She said he probably died.

She told me the story so nonchalantly that it shocked me, but death in remote Haiti is quite common. In that part of Haiti, I was told that five out of six children die before the age of eighteen. It's a death zone that most of the world knows and cares nothing about. I would sadly learn later in my travels that Haiti doesn't have exclusivity on those types of statistics.

For part of the first day there, we toured the facilities. As we walked around, I noticed guards with sawed-off shotguns and automatic weapons positioned around the compound. I learned about all the ministries that took place there. Every morning they opened the steel gates that protected the compound and let in a couple of hundred people. They are offered free food and medical and eye care.

There was also an orphanage inside the compound for babies up to three years old. They offered food programs for the locals. They also had an orphanage for special needs children and housing for geriatric people.

As we continued our tour around the huge compound, we signed out baby orphans like you would check out a book in a library. They did this so the babies would get some human interaction and touch. My baby was extremely sick. He had snot pouring out of his nose and was coughing and crying the entire time I held him. Shamefully I was very eager to put him back in his crib when the time came. I marveled at how my traveling companion, Cameron, a seasoned missionary, delighted in every minute of carrying and loving on one of these cadaverous babies. Cameron is one of those people who has learned to dispense love and compassion freely.

The first night at the mission I couldn't sleep. We laid down in a concrete, masonry block building that was unpainted and unfinished. The buildings inside of the compound were protected by large coils of barbed wire on top of the surrounding walls. None of the window openings in the building I slept in were finished. They were just rough holes of punched-out blocks.

During our tour earlier that day one of the head nurses told me to stay "sprayed up." She said the mosquitoes that bite you during the day give you typhoid, while the mosquitoes that bite you at night give you malaria. So before retiring for the night I bathed myself with mosquito spray!

I wanted to journal so badly that night as it was only 10 p.m. and I wasn't ready to sleep yet. Ten p.m., though, is when they turn their generators off and there is no more electricity. It gets extremely dark out when there are no lights for miles. I turned on my flashlight so I could write, but that turned out to be a big mistake. In seconds there were hundreds of mosquitoes and bugs swarming around my head, so I turned it off immediately. I lay there listening to the ominous rhythm of the voodoo drums beating in the distance. It was the Haitian's litany to the Devil. It was the first time in my life that I felt with such certainty the presence of evil. It's impossible to describe, but it seemed like a type of darkness entered the building that was darker than the night itself. It was so unmistakable that I felt I could touch it. I lay there shaking in fear, more frightened than I had ever been in my entire life.

The following day was Sunday, and we attended a church across the street from the mission compound. I noticed something odd. Several of the women slept through the service and I wondered if it was some sort of a Haitian custom. After the service, I learned it was because in that part of Haiti many of the homes have dirt floors upon which their occupants sleep. During the rainy season, which was while we were there, it would rain throughout the night. The rains would leak through the roofs and from under the walls. The water flowed through the dirt floors, turning them to mud and the children would get wet. To prevent this the mothers held their children in their arms standing up all night under a dry part of the roof. That's why they slept in church. They would put the babies in the nursery and then collapse from exhaustion and get an hour or two of sleep during the service.

Later that day we walked around the town and down to the marketplace which was held on an old riverbed. I had heard of something called "mud cookies" before, but now I got to see them in person. They were used to ease constant hunger and were sold three for a nickel. They definitely were not my mom's cookie recipe!

I was told, that to make them, you take a bottle of vegetable oil and mix it with dirt. Then you pat the mud mixture into small pancake-shaped cookies and lay them on the hot concrete to dry.

How hungry do you have to be before you eat dirt? I hoped I would never learn that answer.

A day or so later we visited what is referred to as the "Far West." It's only about thirty miles from the mission's compound but it is more than a three-hour drive. First, we had to drive through hordes of people walking down the middle of the streets in Port-de- Paix, and then onto some of the most rugged, poorly defined dirt roads, I have ever traveled on. Our drive there was extremely challenging. At one point we drove through a flowing river about one hundred yards wide and a couple of feet deep because there were no bridges in that part of Haiti. There I saw many naked people bathing or washing the only piece of clothing they might own.

Arriving in the "Far West" was like landing on another planet. It had vast regions of desert-like conditions with only dirt prairies, scrub brush, and thorny bushes for miles.

We reached a very small village where we saw women returning from the water well, located about two miles away from the village. They were carrying five-gallon buckets of water that weighed forty pounds each. They did that twice a day.

I took a picture of one of the ladies who was carrying water back to her village. She looked weather-beaten and tough.

"Why do all the people have such angry looks on their faces?" I asked one of the missionaries.

"That's not the face of anger. It's the look of hopelessness."

I'll never forget that look. They were the eyes of zombies, dead and distant.

"The eyes of hopelessness cannot be fixed with just prescription lenses," I thought to myself.

Only a few families lived in this village in mud huts with straw roofs. Inside their homes would be very little or even no furniture at all. This took my definition of poor to a whole new level. I think back to this whenever I use the phrase "Haiti poor."

It was here I was introduced to a young missionary couple who had recently built a small house in this God-forsaken barren wasteland. They were only in their twenties, but they were light-years ahead of me spiritually and had already fully dedicated their lives to comforting the poor. The young missionary told me stories of extraordinary hardships, but also of breakthroughs and God-sized victories.

They took us swimming in the Atlantic Ocean in a beautiful cove that was only a few hundred yards away from their home. The ocean vistas were stunning. I couldn't help but think that back in the States this land would sell for millions of dollars per acre, but here it was almost uninhabited. It was so impoverished that no one wanted to live there.

"I have to return here. I must help these people see," I thought to myself. I knew that one day I would be back again.

On our way back to base camp, we detoured to a small community called Beauchamp. We drove on dirt roads full of bowling-ball-sized jagged rocks, and our truck popped a tire. We were literally in the middle of nowhere. Thank God, we had a spare tire and some of the Haitians traveling with us quickly and gladly changed it for us.

While we were waiting I found a little doll figure with cloth wrapped around it. One of the missionaries told me that it was something voodoo priests used in their rituals. He pointed to the small house next to where our tire exploded. He said it belonged to a voodoo priest. He knew this because of the flags that were hanging from the home. The whole thing was creepy and I was glad to start moving again.

A few days later we flew back to Port-au-Prince. There I met a pastor named Roro. Pastor Roro helped run a school and was trying to set up a medical center on the school compound. He was also trying to build a medical center in the southwest part of Haiti five hours away in the village of Peredo. It is a small village that you will never find on a map. The next day we went there.

We stopped at a gas station along the way so Roro could fill the tank. He disappeared inside a small building for a moment to pay for the gas and grab us something to eat. During this time, a small group of a half dozen young children saw that we were Americans, and they began pounding loudly on the doors and windows of our car shouting.

"*Give me dollar! Give me dollar!*" they shouted over and over.

When Roro returned, he handed me a sandwich. I took one bite. I didn't care for the taste of it at all. Bread filled with a slice of warm, slimy, disgusting tasting meat was not appealing. I gagged and quietly spit it out.

I rolled my window down an inch or two and handed it to the smallest boy that had been banging on the car. He immediately stuffed the entire sandwich in his mouth so that no one bigger than him would steal it. His face lit up. He was happy to have something to eat even if it was only a sandwich that had a disgusting taste to me.

The roads at the beginning of this trip were fine, but the last part of the five-hour drive was challenging as we had to drive through several rivers and endure very bumpy dirt roads. Again and again, we drove slowly through communities of small shacks and extreme poverty. The journey ended when we drove through dense vegetation and several more creeks until we reached a clearing in the woods where the medical center was to be built.

That night we listened to many of Roro's stories as we feasted on Dinty Moore stew. It was a delightful break from the white rice we had eaten for all our previous meals. I hadn't eaten Dinty Moore since I was in college and had very little money. I remembered it as being rather nasty, but that night I thought it was a meal fit for a king. It's funny how mission trips can quickly change your perceptions.

After spending the night there, we traveled back north to a place called Christian City. It was a small community founded by a missionary group many decades earlier. It was here that I finally met Dr. Ryan. Ryan was a young man who had recently graduated from optometry school and felt the Lord wanted him to spend his first couple of years as a doctor volunteering in the mission field. His skills offered a lot of help to the people in the community there.

He walked us around the entire compound. Then he took me to his simple eye clinic. The lab there was in great disarray compared to optical labs found in the States. It was there that I first met an optician named Frank.

I spent the next day helping Frank repair some of the broken equipment in the lab and organizing things. While doing so I realized that many of the lenses he had ordered from me had gone unused. Some of the prescription lenses were shoved into messy drawers while others were scattered around on various counters. There were easily thousands of dollars worth of lenses that had never been finished or dispensed to patients.

When I asked Frank about this, he just replied that the patients never came back for them. I thought about all the time, effort, and expense I went through to produce those lenses and they just ended up scattered around this disorganized optical lab. I was very upset, but I kept my disappointment to myself. I figured it would do no good to start screaming at someone I just met.

In the optical dispensary, almost all the frame boards were empty. There may have been only five or six frames left on those boards. I counted the total number of spots available and there was room for five hundred frames. I began to think that maybe I could help fill those empty spots. If the boards were filled patients might order a frame they liked and be willing to return and pick them up. My lenses would be put to good use instead of just laying around, unused and scattered randomly in a messy optical lab. I left there upset with everything Frank had done with my lenses but I kept my frustration to myself.

On the last night before we left for the States, we returned to the guest house in Port-au-Prince where we had spent our first night in Haiti. This time, however, Cameron and I were treated to a room without any other strangers in it. We even had a fan. I was learning to become grateful for little blessings like these.

After dinner that evening, I met a pastor from somewhere else in the US. He had finished his mission trip and was also heading back home to the States. We spent the evening recounting our adventures. He told me that he had bought some of those mud cookies I mentioned earlier. He said he was curious as to how they tasted. He then informed me that he vomited after the second bite.

He told me that one Saturday night, while he was there, he went to a Voodoo ritual. I thought he must have been nuts to do that, but he said he just had to know what happened during those rituals. He said that while drums played, he saw the high voodoo priest hold a baby up above his head while saying words the pastor couldn't understand. He said the priest repeated something three times, took a sword, and impaled the baby with it. The pastor said he ran out of there immediately.

If you ask any officials in Haiti if human sacrifices take place, the answer is "absolutely not." Animals might get sacrificed, but not humans, but this pastor told me otherwise. Was he telling the truth? I can't say, I wasn't there, but I had no reason not to believe him. The thought of sacrifices, be they animal or human, throughout many parts of Haiti sent chills through me.

Ephesians 6:12 says, *"For we wrestle not against flesh and blood, but against principalities, against powers, against the rulers of the darkness of this world, against spiritual wickedness in high places."*

Some things in Haiti are concrete proof of the truth of this verse. I learned some things that happen on mission trips are hard to believe. Some things are so bizarre that most people in the States probably would never believe them so I do not usually include them when I share about my God's Eyes trips.

The next day we were to fly back to Miami and then home. This was when Delta had no dedicated terminal in Haiti. Crowds pushed and shoved trying to get into the airport and to the ticket counter. For $30 you could hire a "pusher" and have someone bulldoze you through the line, and take you up to the counter in front of all the people ahead of you. Many of those people had spent an hour or more in line waiting. These pushers would then split the money with the people at the counter. I was tired from the trip and after I spent well over an hour in line watching so many people jump ahead of me, I was done.

Haiti and all its ways had finally worn me completely out. I didn't want to be in Haiti any longer. I couldn't wait until the wheels of the jet lifted off the runway.

When I arrived back in Miami, I knelt in the terminal and kissed the floor. I was so happy just to be back in America.

Some people and missionaries I know love Haiti, but I'm not one of them. I knew that one day I'd go back, but if it was up to me it wasn't going to be anytime soon. I knew that there was plenty of work to be done there and I kept thinking about all those empty spots on the frame boards. At the same time, however, I easily convinced myself that it all could wait.

I wanted to share stories about my trip to Haiti with all my friends, but once again no one was interested in listening to them except my wife. Even the people and staff members at my church were not interested. I was learning that this journey into missions was going to be a lonely one.

Chapter Eight
THE LEAP

After my first few mission trips, I continued to run my businesses full-time and served God only part-time. I grew increasingly dissatisfied with my existence. I felt God nudging me to give Him not only my vacation time but all my other time as well, especially after I had to cancel two God's Eyes trips due to employee staffing problems.

This toe-dipping into missions was exciting in many ways. For the first time in my life, I began to feel an intimacy developing with God I had never felt before. I realized the experiences of helping people who desperately needed help were beginning to bring me joy and a greater purpose in life. However, amidst this excitement, doubt also crept in. The same haunting realizations that something big would have to change, returned. Common sense questioned me constantly. There was simply not enough time in my life to travel all around the world. My work consumed most of my time. I had a large income, and with that came large responsibilities. I couldn't just walk away from the obligations I had. How could I keep both my career and be a full-time missionary? Wasn't I already doing enough? I justified that since I felt like I was doing more than most of the people in my church did, maybe this leap never really needed to be made. There was just no way, I reasoned, that I could do more than I was already doing. Making the transition into full-time mission work, even though I felt that I should, would be impossible.

I began talking to my wife about it. I wanted to talk with the head pastor at my church, but he was far too busy with church business and had no time for personal chats. Two of our assistant pastors had secular careers before becoming pastors so I thought they might be good resources for me. I spoke with them separately and they both told me the same thing.

"Just do it," they said, "God will provide a way for everything to work out."

They encouraged me, saying they both made the transition and they had never looked back. I wanted to step out, but I doubted I had their level of faith. My own abilities would only take me so far. I needed more faith in God. God's Eyes was growing, and more missionary eye doctors wanted help. I also felt compelled to go back to the places I had already been to and help more people. But how could I pull it off? I had already seen God show up and begin to supply things for the ministry, but unless I had the funding in hand to be able to close my businesses, how could I ever make "The Leap"?

That week I had a dream about a storm. The short version of that dream is this. I was standing on the roof of an extremely tall building, perhaps hundreds of stories high. A humongous storm was approaching, one of which the world had never seen before. One where earthquakes, tornadoes, and tsunamis were all combined into one. They were about to hit the building I was perched on. I knew this storm would cause the building to collapse. Out of nowhere, a pair of large white wings appeared but they stopped 30 feet short of the building. I knew the wings came to rescue me. They spoke to me and told me to leap. But it was an impossible leap; the wings were just too far away.

… AND THE DREAM SUDDENLY ENDED.

WHEN I AWOKE, I DIDN'T KNOW WHAT EVERYTHING in the dream was about, but I started to feel an urgency to take action and make a leap of faith that seemed impossible to do. If I didn't take it, it seemed as though everything I had built my life upon would collapse.

This all tied into my struggle with whether I would trust God enough to be able to do what He was asking me to do. He wanted me to not only surrender control of my finances but also my career and my time as well.

There's a verse in Matthew 19 which says, *"With man things are impossible, but with God all things are possible."*

AFTER THIS DREAM, THERE WAS A GROWING PART of me that began to believe that if I gave up my desires to always be comfortable and to obtain the finer things in life, I was sure that God would honor that. I would then have all the time I needed to go on mission trips and serve the poor.

However, there was also still a part of me that wanted nothing at all to do with leaping full-time into missions. I was constantly questioning God again as to why He would even ask me to do such a thing. There were so many better people than me to ask. Many people were better prepared for this kind of life and fully desired to do it.

Even after seeing God do things in my life, I realized if I was being completely honest with myself I didn't want to do mission work full-time at all. Deep inside though I knew I should move forward. The time had come for a leap of faith, rather than just baby steps. I had to stop walking on both sides of the fence. I knew I should move beyond the comfortable lukewarm Christian life to which I had become so accustomed. I just wanted it to be easier.

I approached my wife Jenn with the idea that I was seriously considering giving up my businesses and going into missions full-time.

"What do you think about that?" I asked.

"Have you considered all the ramifications?" she asked.

"Yes, you know I've been wrestling with it every night for the past two years. Do you want to know all the possible scenarios I've considered?"

"No, just give me your conclusion."

"Well, I feel this strong calling on my life to make this leap into missions, and other than selfish reasons, I can't think of any good excuses for not doing it."

"Well, what will happen if we can't afford our mortgage payment?"

"I'm fairly certain that if we don't make the mortgage payments eventually the bank will foreclose on us and take our house away."

"What would we do then?" she queried.

"We would have to move to a smaller house in a less expensive town where your salary alone would allow us to live."

"Well, if that's all that would happen, then I don't know why you wouldn't leap."

That was not the answer I had hoped for. I was hoping that she would have fussed about it and told me, it was a dumb idea.

What kind of woman tells her husband to quit his job to follow God and possibly become poor? I was fortunate enough to be married to a woman who loves Father more than things. Secretly, though I wanted her to be the one who would return me to my correct senses. I thought that way I would have been able to save face in front of Father. I could have said something like Adam did when he was confronted:

"You know I wanted to do the things you wanted me to, Lord, but that woman you gave me ...."

If she would have only put up a little bit of a fuss, I would have been able to retain my spiritual pride in being a good Christian. She didn't resist, and I was all out of excuses. Other than desiring money and the comfort it provided, I had no reasons left not to do it.

Matthew 6:24 reminded me:
"No one can serve two masters, for either he will hate the one and love the other, or he will be devoted to the one and despise the other. You cannot serve God and money."

ONE NIGHT I FELT MY TIME WAS UP. IT WAS TIME TO make a choice. Just like the time in the book of Joshua when he asked the people of Israel to choose that very day who they were going to serve. Would I choose to serve the God who had good plans for my life, the God who loved me so much he was willing to offer me love and forgiveness which I didn't deserve? Or would I choose to follow the gods of money, success, and comfort? I wanted more time, but that night I felt a choice had to be made. I knew that when you jump off a building there's no going back but, somehow in the middle of that night, I chose to....

LEAP!

I thought again of Joshua in the Bible and declared to myself as he did. *"As for me and my house, we will serve the Lord."*

IT WAS OVER. I FINALIZED THE DECISION. THERE was no pomp and circumstance, no amazing spiritual experience, only a quiet decision deep inside my heart. I would close my businesses and go full-time into ministry work. I would leap from being a believer into becoming a disciple.

Chapter Nine
DRESS FOR SUCCESS

Just as I hoped Father would do, when my money ran out, checks to fund God's Eyes started appearing in my mailbox. Some were from friends, but many from people I never knew and from States, I had never even been to. Companies began to call us, asking if they could donate products. People and churches started calling us, asking us to come on trips with them to help people see, and offering to pay all our expenses.

One such lady was Martha who called me out of the blue one day. Martha lived in the States but grew up in a small town high up in the mountains of Peru. She asked me if I would go to Peru with her. Most of the people in her hometown were poor and they needed help. Martha's family, however, was wealthy. She had been fortunate enough to attend college in the United States where she met and fell in love with a young brilliant American doctor. They married and spent most of their time in the U.S., but Martha frequently traveled back to her roots. She had a huge heart for the people from her village. She offered to pay my expenses on the trip and told me she was leaving in ten days. I told her there was no way I could make all the lenses I would need for a trip in just ten days.

"Bring whatever you can, but you need to bring eye drops. Many of the poor in my town must work in mines. Their eyes get irritated from all the dust and dirt in those mines," she told me.

"Martha, I'm sorry but I don't supply eye drops. I only supply eyeglasses."

She continued speaking as though she didn't hear me.

"You need to come and bring eye drops!" she insisted.

"Martha, thank you for the invite but I'm not even sure if God wants me on this trip. I promise you that I will pray about it and that I'll call you back in one or two days."

That evening I ran it past Jennifer. She reminded me that we had been praying about where I was to go next and seeing that my expenses were going to be covered, she felt this was simply God answering our prayers and she felt that I should go. I, however, wanted even more confirmation before making that decision. So, we prayed and asked Father to give me additional confirmation about whether I should go. Besides I had no idea where I could get large amounts of eye drops from.

The very next day another woman called me.

"I work for an ophthalmology practice, and we've recently learned about God's Eyes. I wanted to know if we can donate some frames to you all," she asked.

"Sure! "You can do anything that God is telling you to do." It was my standard reply.

Then she asked, "Can you also use eye drops?"

"Eye drops? Well, I guess I'm going to Peru…," I mumbled.

"What?" she said.

"Yes, as of yesterday I can use eye drops."

It was the confirmation I was looking for. An anonymous call offering me the required eyedrops for the trip secured the plan. I called Martha and told her I would go. During the week before we left, another ophthalmology practice also offered me more eye drops. Before we left on that trip, over 500 vials of eye drops were donated to us and, during that ten-day trip, we handed them all out.

In Peru, we spent the first night at Martha's condominium in Lima. She told us to be all packed up and ready to leave for the mountains at 7 a.m. sharp the next morning. We were all ready, but none of the Peruvians were. I quickly learned there is no need to ever wear a watch in Peru, except for decoration. Nothing takes place on time, and that is the norm. We sat around for nearly eight hours before leaving around 3 p.m. that afternoon. We later joked that *morning* in Peru means sometime before the sun sets and *evening* just means, well, whenever.

The journey to the village we were going to could be dangerous so Martha hired six armed bodyguards for the trip. There were two armed guards in each of the three trucks we used for travel. From Lima, it was to be an eight to twelve-hour drive high up into the Andes Mountains. Due to our late start, we didn't reach our destination until late at night.

I traveled in the middle truck of that caravan. The last truck, however, needed to take a short detour to pick up Martha's husband, Kevin, at the airport. A few miles after separating from us, carjackers stopped the truck, overpowered the bodyguards and it was quickly stolen. It contained many of our suitcases including the one containing all my clothing. Also stolen were boxes filled with Bibles. I wonder what the looters did with them. Perhaps it was all part of God's plan for their distribution.

We didn't know, until later, that any of this happened. All we knew was that the truck never arrived that night.

Once you leave sea level and head up into the Andes your ascent is rapid. We went from sea level to 15,000 feet in only a few hours. Unfortunately, the quick ascent introduced me to altitude sickness for the first time in my life. My head felt like it was going to explode. High up in the mountains we stopped and pulled off the road in the middle of nowhere so one of the girls, also suffering from it, could vomit. I got out of the truck as well and lay down on what they called "the highway" holding my pounding head. One of the bodyguards ran over to me quickly.

"Bryan, you cannot lie here. You may get hit by a truck!" he shouted.

"I want to be hit by a truck," I responded.

I was so nauseous, and my head hurt so bad I had no idea how I was ever going to continue. Once you get altitude sickness the only way to get rid of it is to go to a lower elevation or wait a few days until your body acclimates to the altitude. I had to do the latter. A couple of days later I did begin to slowly feel better as I rested. They loaded me up with the local Matta tea used for such a malady. If someone opened an oxygen bar up there, they could make a fortune off people visiting from the US.

After I had recuperated, Martha took us to an orphanage. It appeared nice from the outside, but the inside was quite a different story. Those poor kids lived locked up, from the outside world, in messy housing with horrible odors. The orphanage was so poor they couldn't afford to turn the lights on at night. As soon as the sun went down, the kids all had to go to bed. I just knew I had to hold an eye clinic there one day. A couple of years later we did exactly that!

Since the suitcase containing my clothes was stolen, I only had a few pieces of clothing to change into. After a day or two, I ran out of clean clothes.

A few days later we came across a roadside shack that had T-shirts and shoes for sale. I bought an extra-large shirt because the people who live that high up in the Andes are very small. Their average height is only five feet tall. They had never even heard of a shoe size eleven, so I couldn't buy any shoes. It turned out that the shirt I bought was way too small for me as well, but I desperately needed something fresh to wear to church since my suit and dress shoes had been stolen. When Sunday came and I got all dressed up in my old tennis shoes and the only clean shirt I had, the tiny, supposedly extra-large, T-shirt that I had bought.

The church we attended was extremely small, maybe seating only 40 people. The custom there was for women to sit on one side of the church while the men sat on the other. As visitors, we were seated in the front row. Since my Spanish is extremely limited, I asked Martha if there would be a translator there so I could understand the sermon.

"Yes, of course!"

"Who will be giving the sermon?" I asked.

"You are!" Martha said.

Then she continued, "Why are you wearing a T-shirt with that design on it? That is the symbol for the Inca Devils!"

So, there I was, about to give my first sermon ever with only two minutes to prepare and I was wearing a black satanic-print T-shirt that looked like a midriff on my exposed belly. Yes, indeed, I was certainly dressed for success. I must have looked ridiculous!

The church people were so nice and kind to me. They didn't put me on YouTube, laugh at me, or stone me afterward.

Later that day we held an eye clinic in that tiny church. Even though only forty people could sit in the church, over a hundred people showed up for eyeglasses. When I finished that evening, several tiny old church ladies were still there. They were so grateful for the miracle of sight that they all tightly embraced me and cried in gratitude.

"*Jesus Cristo, Jesus Cristo,*" they'd say to me.

"No, no, no, I'm not Him. He sent me here, but I'm not Him," I'd tell them.

We handed out glasses and eye drops all week to anyone who needed them. We even had extra drops leftover so I donated them to a local Peruvian doctor for future distribution.

Other than altitude sickness, the stolen suitcases, having a very limited wardrobe consisting of a few extra-small clothes, and preaching off the cuff, in a satanic T-shirt, the trip was wonderful. Peru and its people are so incredibly beautiful, especially the vistas from high up in the Andes Mountains. What strikes you about the Peruvians is how amazingly kind they are. Once again, I believed that one day I would return there. Those orphans were on my mind.

Chapter Ten
MARTA

I had been happily married for several years, but one year someone else also captured my heart. She was a little angel in Nicaragua, and her name was Marta.

Our group was working with a medical team from a church in Georgia. We traveled to a very small village to attend a church service on top of a mountain far above the town below. The road was very rough with large potholes and, eventually, it turned to dirt and then to mud.

We arrived on Sunday morning and sat down in this tiny two-light bulb, non-air-conditioned church. The pews were simple wooden benches with no backs. The church could accommodate perhaps eighty people at the very most.

I sat about halfway back on a bench by myself. As the local villagers began to file in, a little girl, about eleven years old, came and sat right next to me even though the rest of the pew was completely empty. In my broken Spanish, I managed to ask her name.

"Cómo te llamas?"

"Marta," she smiled.

Then she did something very unexpected. She rested her head against my shoulder, the same way my daughter did when she was young.

It was early in the morning, and Marta and I were sitting by ourselves. The church was filled halfway to capacity with poor, modestly dressed villagers and I

Marta wearing one of the outfits God's Eyes bought for her from the USA.

We held a God's Eyes clinic on the porch of this shack helping over 100 people to see clearly.

had a little girl's head on my shoulder. This made me somewhat uncomfortable, as I felt my heart beginning to melt.

The service was long and very boring to me since I didn't understand much Spanish. I reached into my backpack, pulled out my iPad and I taught Marta how to play a video game called "Angry Birds." Marta quickly excelled at the game and soon she was winning. I had to keep gesturing to her to be quiet because she would laugh and giggle every time she won a game. After a while, I put away my iPad because some of the other kids wanted to join in and we were becoming a distraction to the pastor.

We had behaved ourselves for a few minutes when I reached into my backpack and pulled out my journal and began to draw pictures of animals and other simple objects. I would quietly whisper to Marta, asking her how to properly say the name of the picture in Spanish. Then she would draw a picture and I would whisper back to her how to pronounce it in English. We spent the rest of the service having fun. We couldn't have come from more different worlds. We had absolutely nothing in common except for being completely bored in church.

When the long service finally ended, I began to put my journal away, but Marta gestured that she wanted to keep my pen and notebook. I wanted to keep it to myself so I could record my thoughts, prayers, and experiences on that trip, but I just couldn't say no to her. I realized this eleven-year-old girl had never had a notebook before. I gave it to her along with my pen and she had me write my name on the first page.

The next morning, we returned to that village on top of the mountain to hold a free medical and eye clinic at the church. When I got off the bus there was a crowd of people who had gathered waiting for our services. Marta was there and when she saw me, she ran up and hugged me. She gestured that she wanted to show me something. She opened the notebook and there was a picture of a man holding a small girl's hand with the inscription "Marta loves Bryan" in Spanish. In less than twenty-four hours, she had successfully won her way into my heart.

Every day she would come back to the clinics. Even though members from our group had activities for the kids to do while their parents waited in line for hours, Marta would sit all day in a chair near to where I was seeing patients. She would smile every time our eyes made contact. This scenario repeated itself day after day.

One night we stayed at the church late into the evening. The pastor wanted to hold an evening baptism service for all the people who committed themselves to follow the teachings of Christ during the week we were there. Quite a large crowd gathered that evening and over one hundred people crowded inside until there was standing room only. The pastor had all of our team sit up on the stage. Marta came up and sat with me for the entire service. I'm not sure what was said, but the service went on for a couple of hours. Several people came forward that evening and they were baptized in a very dirty concrete pit filled with murky water. I wasn't certain that even the promise of salvation would have tempted me to be baptized in it.

There was a lot of celebrating that night and I met Marta's family. The pastor had let me know that Marta's family was extremely poor, and her father drank quite heavily and frequently. I was told she lived in a ridiculously small shack with her parents and seven siblings. The floor of their home was made from dirt. It only had one bed so the children slept on the floor.

After the service, the pastor forbade us to go down the mountain by ourselves. It was dark outside, and he was afraid we might be robbed or assaulted. Many gangs lived on the mountain, and they gathered every day after dark. He called the police for us and we waited until they arrived to escort us. One of the armed officers rode in our bus while the others drove in vehicles both ahead of us and behind us. It made me question how safe life was for little girls like Marta.

On the last day of that trip, we were at a granary at the bottom of the hill the little church was perched upon. We were buying rice, corn, sugar, and flour in large fifty-pound and one hundred-pound bags. We repackaged the staples into smaller five-pound bags. We planned to donate the food to the pastor who would then distribute it to the people in his community.

THEY SHALL SEE GOD

While we were doing this, Marta walked down the hill to us. It was a few-mile walk for her. She walked through fields and wooded areas while proudly wearing her white patent leather high-heeled shoes which were about an inch too big. She had heard we were down there, and she came all that way just to say goodbye to me. When I saw her shoes, I asked why she wore them, and she said it was the only pair she owned.

Near the granary, there was a market, similar to one of our flea markets in the States. Marta and I walked over and found a small booth that sold shoes. I bought Marta three new pairs of shoes and six pairs of socks. Since I knew she would have trouble carrying it all back home, I asked the vendor if they had something like a handbag or backpack. He said he had one remaining backpack in the back and he brought it out. It couldn't have been more perfect! It was a Disney Little Princess pink backpack! I bought it immediately.

I asked Marta if there was anything else that she wanted and she answered with a yes. She wanted a Bible that she could read. After searching for a while, I was able to find her a new Bible printed in Spanish. I gave Marta the money I had leftover. She stayed with us that morning until we all left. I still remember waving goodbye from the window of the bus as we pulled away and Marta ran after the bus until she could no longer keep up.

We flew home that day, and I was back at my house late that evening. As I took a warm shower I pondered how difficult Marta's life was. She did not get to take warm showers with her choice of soaps and shampoos. She was able to take a shower only when it rained outside. After my shower, I would be able to lie down and sleep on a nice pillow-topped mattress in a room where I could adjust the temperature in my home to be whatever I wanted it to be. Marta would be going to bed on a filthy woven mat on the hard ground and would have to endure whatever temperature it was outside. There were no bugs in my bedroom because we pay for a service, but Marta would be getting bit by mosquitoes and other insects. Living in my soft comfortable world made me realize even more how difficult her life was.

The following year we returned to Marta's village. Before the trip, I asked my wife and her friends what a twelve-year-old girl would like to wear or own.

They filled up an entire suitcase with clothes and costume jewelry and fun things a little girl would like.

When we reached her village there was a crowd waiting for us like the last time. As I got off the bus, Marta spotted me, ran from the crowd, and leaped into my arms.

It was awesome to see the delight on her face as she opened the suitcase filled with gifts for her. Then she had a surprise for me. She showed me the Bible I had given her a year before. She had filled out the first page with information such as the date she received it and who gave it to her. She showed me that she was reading it and showed me the verses that she had highlighted during the year. I was proud of her.

The rest of the days of the trip were like the first trip. Marta spent almost every day sitting near me as I examined peoples' eyes and made them eyeglasses. On our last day in that village, Marta once again walked down the mountain to say goodbye. This time her mother and one of her sisters accompanied her. I bought them lunch and just before it was time for our team to leave, Marta's mother wanted to tell me something.

I located a translator and Marta's mother softly grabbed Marta by her shoulders and placed her in front of me.

"You take Marta home with you," she said.

There is nothing greater than the love of a mother. She was willing to live without ever seeing her daughter again, just so Marta might have a better life. My heart broke. Both of us had eyes that welled up with tears as I tried my best to explain why it would not be possible to take Marta with me.

As our bus pulled away Marta once again chased after it until she could no longer keep up. Little did I know that would be the last time I would ever see Marta.

The following year our God's Eyes team did not return to her village, but the medical team did. One of the medical team members transcribed a letter from Marta and gave it to me when she got back to Georgia. Marta said she was very sad that I didn't come that year and she wrote how much she missed me and that she loved me and hoped that next year we would see each other.

Her last sentence said, "Please pray for me because I am sick." I never knew what she meant by sick. My mind was anguished over whether she just had something like a cold or whether it was something more severe than that.

The next year I did return to Nicaragua and after a few days of holding eye clinics there, I became terribly ill. I vomited nonstop for a couple of days. As I began to feel better, we drove a few hours south to Marta's village, and we drove up the mountain to where she lived. I could barely contain my joy because I was going to see her again! I imagined Marta once again running up to the bus and jumping into my arms, but when I got off the bus, she wasn't there. I thought maybe she might be in school and that she would certainly show up later.

We started our eye clinic as I impatiently awaited her arrival. I waited all day and she never showed up. Finally, I asked the pastor about her. He told me that sometime before we arrived Marta's mother took the children and moved away. He said no one knew where they moved to. They were there one day and then gone the next, and they had left in a hurry. I asked him whether he thought they would return, and he said he didn't know because some of their belongings were still in the shack. I gave him money to give to Marta and her mother if they ever returned and he said he would do that. I also left him every bit of contact information I had just in case he ever found out where they were. I never heard from the pastor and I never saw Marta again.

For quite some time I couldn't keep my mind from thinking I should have made plans and done whatever was necessary for Jenn and me to adopt Marta and bring her to the U.S. so we could get her out of her bad situation. I never did and now it is too late.

Sometimes we miss opportunities to do the right thing, and we never get another chance to correct it. The truth was that I was too selfish to take on another child. I had many logical excuses. I was already fifty-five years old, and I didn't want to raise another child. I failed Marta, and I failed Father. I believe that families who adopt children are the best people on the planet. I am not one of those people. That was nearly eight years ago, and I know I have been forgiven for my lack of love and compassion, but sometimes I am still haunted and ashamed of the way I responded.

MANY CHILDREN HURT AND CRY. THOSE CRIES ARE never heard and therefore, those children are never helped. I regret that I missed out on all the joy that comes from adopting a child and doing the good works I was created to do. I was just too full of lame excuses. I had started to care way too late.

All of us know that there are millions of children like Marta. Why do we just turn our eyes and ears away from them whenever they come along? Why do logical excuses override the calls from our hearts?

Isaiah 65:19 says:

"The voice of weeping shall be no more heard in her, nor the voice of crying." I pray that happens one day for Marta.

Chapter Eleven

A RECURRING TEMPTATION

When I finally committed to going into full-time Christian work, I clearly remembered the day when I finally closed my lab and had everything packed up and moved. I walked out of my former office to my car and before I even started the engine, I immediately called this great guy I had met while on my first mission trip.

He was the head fundraiser of a large medical mission group and had previously offered to help me out. He had achieved remarkable success for his nonprofit group. He successfully encouraged existing donors to contribute substantially more, and they were bringing in several millions of dollars every year. I knew that he was gifted at what he was doing. We kept in contact, and I thought he would be the ace up my sleeve I needed if I ever made the leap.

"Just let me know when you are ready, I can walk you through the steps on how to get funding," I remembered him telling me. The day I closed down the lab I called him immediately.

"I did it! I shut down my optical lab and I'm ready to do this mission work full-time. I need your wisdom and your input. What's the first thing I need to do ?"

"The very first thing you need to do is to notify everyone on your donor list and let all your donors know that you have gone into full-time ministry."

"All my donors?" "I don't have any donors." The truth was I had a couple of them, but very few.

"What? You don't have any donors!"

"No, basically, it's only me."

Then he said the words that I will never forget.

"Well, if you don't have any donors, then I can't help you," he said.

I almost jumped out of the car and ran back into the office to plead with the landlord for my space back. My heart sank. The ace up my sleeve was worthless. It would only be me and Father now. I never felt so sad in my whole life. I drove home not knowing what to do or how we would ever survive. I felt I had just made a huge mistake.

On another occasion, I was tempted to use a professional fundraiser. I was spending the weekend in Northern Mississippi, and I met a man there named Mike and we started to have a conversation. When I asked him what he did for a living he told me he raised money for nonprofits. Hmmm … I instantly thought this must be a divine appointment of some kind. I told him that I had started a nonprofit organization, and I sure could use the funding for it. We chatted for a while and before he left, he invited me to come to visit him at his office headquarters in Memphis, Tennessee. He, too, told me that he thought he could help raise funds for us.

A couple of weeks later my son and I drove to see him. He had a nice setup in a busy office where he was raising money for a large nonprofit organization that helped children in Memphis. He was phenomenally successful in funding it and had already helped raise several hundred thousand dollars in a short time for their annual fundraising campaign. He asked me for specifics about God's Eyes.

"What does it cost to provide a pair of glasses?"

"Where will you be doing work?"

"What is your distribution plan?" And so on.

After an hour of answering his questions and giving him figures and statistics, he said something that surprised me.

"Bryan, companies love stuff like you're doing and there is so much money out there for nonprofits like yours. I'm positive I can get money for you. Heck, just let me know and I could raise you $25,000 by the end of the week and $100,000 by the end of the month. Companies are going to jump all over this. It'll be really easy to raise a lot of money for what you're doing."

Wow, I couldn't believe it! I wanted to jump up and down and high-five everyone I saw. I thought God must have planned this entire meeting for sure. I was so excited.

Then Mike popped my balloon.

"All you've got to do, Bryan, is get rid of that stupid name. I have no idea why you would call it "God's Eyes." Companies don't like to donate to nonprofits that might discriminate on a religious basis. Let's just change the name to "Sight for the Poor" or something simple like that. I love this whole idea of you helping people to see, but I don't understand any of that God stuff you're talking about. Why don't you just think about a couple of new names to call your nonprofit and run them by me next week."

I left feeling both excited and deflated at the same time. The entire reason I was doing this was a God thing. How could I take His name out of everything? God alone was the only reason I even started down this path.

But, receiving $100,000 cash when all my money was dwindling, and having even lots more coming in later sure seemed appealing. I began to rationalize that I could easily change the name and God would still know that my heart's motives were good. I had the following conversation with myself.

"Envision all the additional people You could help!" I told myself. Isn't that the reason for doing this? The poor wouldn't care one bit what the name of the group is so long as they received improved vision … Right?"

Back and forth I waffled on this. But why would I call my nonprofit something other than God's Eyes? Was I considering dropping God's name just to get some money? Why would I ever change the name when I was so positive that we were to call it "God's Eyes" in the first place?

If you ever have trouble sleeping too much, just start a nonprofit organization named God's Eyes. My struggles over the name change caused my sleepless nights to return. I needed to either stop reading my Bible or invest in a good pair of scissors and cut out all those annoying verses like Mathew 10:33, which kept running through my mind.

"Whoever denies me before men, I also will deny before my Father who is in heaven."

I prayed over this for a long time. I ended up calling Mike back, telling him I couldn't change the name thus ending this opportunity.

A THIRD FUNDRAISING OPPORTUNITY FOR ME WAS when another man contacted me. He had stellar credentials for fundraising because he had worked for some of the most well-known and largest Christian ministries that exist today. He helped them raise funds and now he offered to help me. I told him about my convictions about not asking people for money.

"You won't have to. All you must do is invite wealthy people over to God's Eyes for dinner. I'll ask them for you."

It sounded like a bit of a compromise of my convictions, but he had raised millions of dollars for well-known groups. Once again my initial thoughts were that God must have had us cross paths for this very reason.

"Where is your headquarters?" he asked.

"In my spare bedroom and our inventory is stored in my garage and several of my friends' garages," I told him.

"I can't bring investors over to your bedroom or drive them all over town to people's garages! You need to get a headquarters building somewhere."

I knew he was right, but I didn't have enough money to rent a place anywhere. Office and warehouse space in our town was expensive.

I decided to reach out one more time to someone I knew, who was a successful businessman who was well known in local Christian circles. He was involved in the establishment and building of several churches in town. I knew he had connections with other financially successful people like himself. I knew his faith was strong. I thought, in the back of my mind, that he would surely help me and offer to connect me with people who would give generously.

When I talked with him, I asked him for the phone numbers of his wealthy friends, and possible candidates that would invest in my ministry.

Then he gave me some advice that I will never forget.

"Bryan, you've got to decide who's running this ministry that you're talking about. Is it going to be God or are *you* going to run it? If you tell me it's God, then you've got to let him supply. You need to trust in Him. You must have the strongest conviction that He alone is in charge. You don't need my money or my friends' money. You need to learn to trust in God."

I knew he was right. God already taught me that, through the book about George Mueller I had read, but I am a very slow learner. Why did I forget that lesson so quickly?

I knew God alone was in charge and that He would provide. The Creator of the universe needs no assistance. I felt so dumb because of how easily I forgot those lessons when money was being waved in my face. I asked Father to forgive me. I told him I wouldn't hire any fundraisers to raise money.

"Trust in the Lord with all your heart. Lean not on your own understanding: In all your ways acknowledge him and He shall direct all your ways." (Proverbs 3: 5-6)

WHY WOULD I EVEN WANT TO FORGE AHEAD WITHout him? God was in charge. I was learning I needed to get out of His way and to stop trying to take things into my own hands.

Chapter Twelve
ZAMBIA

I received a call one day from a man in South Africa. He told me his name was Francois and that he was one of the African directors of a group called Operation Mobilization (OM). He said he had heard of what God's Eyes was doing and that he wanted me to come to an OM missionary gathering called "The Love Conference." Francois told me that missionaries from all over Africa would be there and he wanted to introduce me to all of them. He hoped that I would eventually visit those countries and host God's Eyes clinics there. He wanted to use us as an evangelistic outreach tool in those countries.

He offered to pay all my ground expenses but added that he would not be able to pay for my airfare.

"How much will the airfare be?" I asked.

"From Atlanta to here I believe is around $2000," he replied.

"I'm sorry, but I don't have that much available for a ticket. But I will pray and see what God thinks." I replied.

Francois called me a few months later.

"How is your fundraising going for the trip?" he asked.

"Well ... we don't do fundraising," I explained.

"Well, Bryan, I need to know if you are coming because I need to make arrangements for you. I can only give you a few more days before I'll need your answer."

"Ok, I will pray about it and get back to you shortly."

And so that's exactly what I did. I prayed.

"Lord, I don't know if you want me to go to Zambia or not, but if you do, then I will need $2000 for airfare. I don't mean to rush, but I have a three-day window for an answer," I told Father.

The next day I went to one of our evening Bible studies. One of the women at the study held up a book she had just finished reading and said it was a great book. She recommended everyone buy a copy of it and read it. After the meeting was over, I asked her if I could borrow her copy. She readily agreed and handed me the book. I took it home that night and placed it on my nightstand.

The next evening my wife returned home from a two-day teaching conference. My wife is a voracious reader, and I knew she would enjoy having another book to read. I told her about the new book I received at the Bible study.

"What is the book about?" Jennifer asked me.

"I really don't know. I'll go to the bedroom and get it."

When I returned, I browsed through the book, told her the name of the book, and read some of the chapter titles. As I was doing that, I found an envelope in the book addressed to God's Eyes. When I opened it, there was a check in the envelope for $2000! I held it up.

"Hey, Jenn, I guess I'm going to Zambia!" I exclaimed.

Once again Father confirmed and supplied.

ODDLY, THE GIRL, WHO LOANED ME THE BOOK, didn't know about the envelope with a check inside of it. We found out later that her brother-in-law, who was a local doctor, had placed the envelope in her book. He told us later that God had spoken to him, told him to write a $2000 check to God's Eyes and to place the check inside his sister-in-law's book.

I traveled to Zambia and so much happened. I flew to Johannesburg, South Africa, on a nonstop sixteen-hour flight, in a window seat of the coach section. As the trip unfolded, I realized that sitting there was a mistake. I remember trying hard not to look at my watch for as long as I could. I watched a few movies before doing so. When I finally looked at my watch, I discovered that I had flown for 8 long hours, and that meant I still had 8 more hours to go.

For me, it was absolute misery. I had spilled an entire large cup of soda all over my lap just after boarding the flight and so I was sitting in wet pants. Then to add to my misery I had had two more sodas during those first eight hours, and I needed to pee badly! Both people next to me, neither of whom I knew, were sound asleep. I couldn't climb over them, and I didn't want to wake them. I tried to sleep, but I couldn't because I was full of caffeine, and I desperately had to use the restroom. I was growing increasingly more uncomfortable by the minute. I squirmed and squirmed and squeezed and squeezed. I sat there for another three hours turning blue, or should I say yellow, in the face until my seatmates woke up to use the bathroom themselves.

It was a practical learning experience. I discovered that is exactly why you never sit in a window seat during a long flight and why smart medallion flyers only book aisle seats.

WHEN I ARRIVED IN JOHANNESBURG I WAS GOING to be picked up by a friend, only he wasn't there. This was back in the day when my cell phone only worked in America, and I didn't have service anywhere else. My friend Todd was unable to reach me to tell me that he would be an hour and a half late. For ninety minutes I walked around the airport wondering not only where my ride was, but if I even knew where the right place to meet him was. It's a funny feeling one has when you realize you might be lost and you're in a foreign country and your phone doesn't work. Indeed, I was a stranger in a strange land. Eventually, Todd did arrive, and somehow, we found each other in an airport larger than that of Atlanta's Hartsfield-Jackson.

We drove about an hour and a half from Johannesburg to Pretoria where Todd and his wife were living and serving as missionaries. It was almost midnight and once we arrived in Pretoria I noticed that Todd would slow down, but never stop at the stoplights. He told me it was too dangerous to stop. If we stopped, our car could be stolen as we were in the carjacking capital of the world.

THEY SHALL SEE GOD

Todd and Heather lived in a nice home in one of the safest gated communities. Every home had fences, gates, and some had security guards. Even with all that protection, they always made sure all their doors were locked to prevent thieves from entering. Thieves had entered Todd's neighbor's house the week before.

The next day we flew to Zambia. Two small vehicles picked us up. Thirteen of us sat crammed into a small SUV meant for seven. Several pieces of luggage and various containers of supplies were also jammed in with us. The rest were piled high on the roof. We looked like the *Beverly Hillbillies*. The SUV Todd and Heather rode in popped a tire from being so overloaded, and it simply aggravated the situation.

I arrived at the "Love Conference" around four hours later and was very tired, but there was an excitement in the air that lifted my spirits. There were hundreds of missionaries from all over Africa assembled to celebrate, worship, and learn about how they could serve more effectively.

The following day we started our eye clinic. We were there to help all the missionaries attending the conference, but many of the local people got in line as well. The word had spread that we were giving away free eyeglasses.

There was nowhere for us to examine people, so they put us in a bread closet in the local missionary's house. It was about six feet wide by nine feet long with many shelves and filled to the ceiling with bread, rolls, and other food for all the people at the conference. We tested hundreds of people's eyes in that closet.

On the first day two brothers, aged fourteen and twenty-one, showed up. They had no money with which to buy glasses and their parents had no money. Their relatives and all the family's friends had no money. They were poor, and the luxury of eyeglasses was far beyond their financial capabilities. Even if they had money, it would be too far of a journey for them to get somewhere that even offered eyeglasses. Both brothers were extremely nearsighted and had never seen clearly before, but this is how much Father loves them: He sent a stranger from nine thousand miles away to give them the glasses that corrected their eyesight and to let them know that the glasses were a gift from Jesus.

Then they left and I never saw them again. I clearly remember how grateful they were when they departed. I then rationalized that I had not come to Africa to be introduced to missionaries, but had come there to give those two brothers new eyeglasses and to tell them how much Jesus cared for them.

ONE EVENING NEAR THE END OF MY TIME IN ZAMBIA a young lady named Lusungu asked if she could talk with me. I told her that tomorrow would be my last day there; however, if she wanted to meet with me an hour before we started seeing patients the next morning, I would be glad to talk with her. The next morning we met around 6:30 a.m. and she began to tell me her story. Her father was a doctor in the nearby town and her mother was a nurse.

"I want to do what you do," she told me.

She had been to college in Johannesburg and had graduated with a degree in Opticianry. She was also licensed in Zambia to examine and dispense eyeglasses, but she could not find anywhere to work. I felt sorry for her and began to think that maybe I could give her some money to help her out, but then I wondered if perhaps Lusungu had been prepared for us to start God's Eyes in Zambia!

"Would your father give you a room in his clinic for you to dispense glasses?"

"Yes," she said, but I wanted to hear that from him directly. I asked her if I could meet him and ask him personally.

She called him and he agreed to meet me in the evening after both of us had finished working.

I asked Lusungu if she would like to serve with me that day, to which she enthusiastically agreed. All day she worked by my side testing patients and fitting them with new glasses. That evening I met with her father, and he confirmed that Lusunga could have a room in his office.

Lusungu was licensed and ready to work and she wanted to help poor people see. No one else would be that qualified to help us. I told Lusungu that she could start and run God's Eyes Zambia. In addition, we would leave her any supplies we had leftover, and I would send more supplies to her after I returned to the States.

It became crystal clear to me that God had this day planned far in advance.

The next morning, we had to leave Zambia. We left very early, around 4 a.m. On the four-hour drive to the airport through the Zambian countryside, I remember looking at the night sky. It was one of the most beautiful I had ever seen. The full moon and millions of stars shone so amazingly bright. Despite all of its poverty, corruption, and hardships, some things in Zambia were exceptionally beautiful.

WHEN I ARRIVED BACK HOME, I BEGAN PRICING OUT how much it would cost to ship supplies to Zambia. I forget the exact price, but it was several thousand dollars. God's Eyes didn't have that much money, so I began to pray that if God wanted optical supplies to get to Zambia, then He would have to make it happen.

A week later I was invited to speak at a Bible study in a town that was around 30 minutes from where I lived. I remember once making a promise to Father that I would go anywhere, anytime, to talk to anyone about what He has done with His ministry of God's Eyes. I readily accepted the invitation.

The host, Denny Debner, greeted me.

"Come on in! Who are you?" he asked cordially.

"I'm the guy who's speaking tonight "

"Oh, I didn't know you were coming."

Apparently, the man who invited me, never told Denny that I was coming. It was a nice evening and I got to share stories of what God's Eyes had been doing, including our new plans to ship optical supplies to Zambia.

After the Bible study was over, Denny came up to me and said that I hadn't even been there for three minutes, and God told him to help me get the supplies to Zambia. Denny was working for Delta Air Lines at that time. He arranged a meeting between Delta's logistics operational manager and me for lunch three days later.

During lunch, I spoke with Daran, the Delta logistics manager.

"I have worked out a plan to ship your supplies to Zambia via Delta Air Lines," he said. "Then, UPS will deliver them to the town that Lusungu lives in … and Delta will pay for everything … everything except the duties and tariffs that Zambia will impose on your shipment. Delta is not allowed to pay for those two things … but since Delta can't pay for that I will pay for it personally."

A week or two later God showed up again. This time a lady from an optometrist's office in Memphis, Tennessee, called me.

"Our doctor here is in his eighties and is finally going to retire."

He had several hundred finished lens blanks. Lens blanks are the raw form of lenses that you use to make prescription eyeglasses. He had tried to sell all his leftover surplus back to the manufacturer from which he purchased them, but they told him they would not buy them back. They said they had heard of a group that he might want to donate them to. They gave him my number at God's Eyes, and he had his secretary call me.

"Can you use the lens blanks?"

"Yes," I answered. "I will turn them into prescription eyeglasses and distribute them to the poor around the world."

"Can you use anything more than lenses that we might have around here?"

"Yes, we can use almost anything."

"Well, I've got an idea, so let me call you back later." And she hung up.

The following day she did, indeed, call me back.

"Would you be willing to drive up to Memphis? The doctor here owns two eye practices in town and he's going to sell everything he can, but he wants you to give it all a look over first. If you can use anything, just put your name on it. If that item doesn't sell, then he will donate it to you. "

I drove to Memphis and met with the elderly doctor. I told him stories for forty-five minutes about what God was doing through God's Eyes.

"After listening to all you've said, I've decided not to sell everything," he said, "but to donate everything to God's Eyes. You can pick it all up in two weeks."

I returned home and checked on truck rentals. The price was outrageously expensive. My church heard that I needed a truck, and they volunteered to let me use the extended fifteen-passenger van used for the children's ministry. If I removed the bench seats, I could fit quite a bit of stuff inside. They also owned a sixteen-foot flatbed trailer they said I could borrow.

I attended a men's Bible study on Friday mornings and the Friday morning before I left, I asked the men if they would pray for me and my son because I was going to drive that large van and trailer to Memphis and I had never driven anything like that before. After the study, a friend came up to me and said that he had calculated how much gas would cost, and he gave me money for that. Another study companion approached me with some money to buy meals. Then when I got home, I had an offer in the mail for a free hotel stay at a resort near Memphis!

My son and I drove to Tennessee and picked up everything we could fit in the van and on the flatbed trailer.

One of the items in his office was rather unique. The doctor told me a story:

"In the Sixties, I had a surprise visit. A man came to my office at closing time. I was just about to walk out and go home because it was five o'clock and I always left the office at five on the dot. My receptionist told me I still had one more patient to see in room one." He paused.

"I was a bit perturbed," he laughed slightly. "It was past closing time, but my receptionist convinced me to see the guy anyway. When I walked into the room, it was Elvis Presley! He was there waiting to get his eyes examined. He was very farsighted. After the exam, Elvis picked out a pair of eyeglasses he liked. He wanted two pairs of the same frame, but I only had one frame in stock. When I called the manufacturer to order the second frame, they told me that the frame style he wanted had been discontinued. 'Well, I said, you better start making them again because Elvis Presley just ordered one.'"

I grinned and nodded. The manufacturer started making that frame again and the doctor told me they sold over a million of them. He became Elvis's eye doctor from then on.

"The blue exam chair you just loaded up was the chair Elvis used to sit in whenever he came in for testing."

I kept that exam chair in my warehouse for a few years and then donated it to a museum.

THE ZAMBIA TRIP MADE A LASTING IMPRESSION ON me as I realized all that Father had done:

- He provided the money for me to go to Zambia.
- He provided a licensed person for us to work with there.
- He provided supplies for us to send there through an eye doctor in Tennessee.
- He provided the vehicle we needed to haul everything back home.
- He provided the money for the gas it took to get everything.
- He provided free food for us while we were on the trip and a free room to stay in.
- He introduced us to Denny who introduced us to Daran who had the status and ability to get Delta to ship our supplies for free and who would pay all of our duty fees and tariffs personally.

God did all of this, and it cost us nothing financially. The only cost was being willing to do it. These are the kinds of things Father does for his ministries. This confirms my belief that if God wants a ministry to exist, He will provide for it. We don't have to solicit money from people, God himself will convict others to get involved to accomplish His will.

Chapter Thirteen
SETTING UP SHOP

After I had closed my optical lab, the ministry began to grow larger and the need came for God's Eyes to get a headquarters somewhere. My friends, who stored supplies for me, were beginning to call me.

"Uh, Bryan, we're glad to help, but how long are you going to keep all your stuff in our garage?"

I was working out of my own garage, as well. The chemicals released while cutting certain lenses gave off a bad odor, and Jenn would occasionally mention how bad the house was smelling.

"It sure would be nice to be able to park a car in our garage again!" she said semi-jokingly.

Additionally, having to constantly drive across town just to pick up supplies from friends' garages was beginning to be very time-consuming and starting to annoy me as well.

I prayed that God would provide a space for us. I looked at the budget for God's Eyes and knew we couldn't afford more than $600 a month for a space, and even that would be stretching it a bit. I also knew that there was no place around that would be big enough for us to set up an optical lab and store all our equipment and supplies for that amount of money. It would take a blessing. I prayed about it and waited for direction. Waiting is so difficult. I realized that waiting on God was one of those things that people with strong faith did well. I was learning to not expect to push a button and get whatever I wanted immediately. However, this is a hard lesson to learn for someone who used to tell his microwave oven to hurry up.

A short time later I was invited by a church to be a part of their mission week. This church did not support us, but they offered to give us a space in their mission hall. I ran into a lady there, Cathy, who ran a large food bank ministry in town. When our sons were young, they were close friends. She invited me to come and tour her ministry, in the next town over, and to check out everything they were doing.

She had a large setup that helped hundreds of less fortunate people every month. They had beautiful, modern offices connected to several warehouses filled with food for the poor and all kinds of donated items for their resale shops. There were volunteers all over the place and I was somewhat envious of the success of her ministry. I mentioned to her that one day I hoped that the Lord would be willing to provide a space for God's Eyes since we had out-grown our place. She said they, too, also needed more space as their ministry continued to grow.

In the units adjacent to hers, a church was renting out office and ware-house space. Cathy thought they might be moving out because they had just completed a large addition on the church property. They wouldn't need to rent the satellite space anymore. She knew the landlord and she also knew he was renting the space for more than double the rent we could afford. Still, she said she would talk to him and see if she could work out a deal for both of us.

They did work out a deal. She received more space, and I secured 700 square feet of finished air-conditioned office space and 1000 square feet of warehouse space for only $600 per month and it was a three-year lease! This was a blessing indeed. There were no facilities anywhere around that could provide that much quality space for anything close to that price. God's Eyes finally had a real headquarters. All our supplies and the optical lab would now be under one roof. My friends and I would soon be able to use our garages to park cars!

I was growing, albeit very slowly, in my faith. I was learning to trust and rely upon Father. I was also learning to wait for His timing. I saw God begin to pour out and supply our ministry's needs. I learned that only Father determines what we do and when we do it and how much we need. God's Eyes was His ministry, not mine. I saw God showing up repeatedly. The more I surrendered control to Him, the more He blessed the ministry.

Denny, whose Bible study I had spoken at previously, visited me at our new location. He told me that he had recently retired from Delta and asked if he could come and learn more about God's Eyes. He said it had been a long time since he had seen God do anything. He was certain that God was showing up at God's Eyes, and he just needed to see that in his life again.

I figured if that's what he wanted to do, it was ok with me. He was a quiet man and didn't speak much those first several days. I told my wife how uncomfortable it was to have a man in my office all day who wouldn't talk. It was like pulling teeth to get Denny to say anything more than monosyllabic responses when I attempted to converse with him.

One day I asked him if he wanted to learn how to cut lenses. He readily agreed and I was relieved. He began to converse more with me. Denny was a quick learner and a hard worker. He became the first full-time volunteer at God's Eyes. We became great friends, and I was delighted when we began to have long, in-depth conversations. Over the next few years, he would become my favorite person to pray with. Since then, we have spent hundreds of hours together in prayer over God's Eyes.

Once, after receiving fourteen pallets of donated new frames, Denny informed me that we were running out of warehouse space and that we had no shelving left.

"We need to go out and buy more shelving," he told me.

"What we need to do Denny, is pray to God to either send us shelving or money to buy shelving," I replied.

"You have some money in the God's Eyes account, and we need the shelving immediately because we have no place to unpack and organize the frames," Denny said.

"None of the money in the account was designated to buy shelving when the donations were made. Let's just pray and wait and see what God wants to do."

I think Denny probably thought I made no sense, but he was willing to go along with it. By the next week, some checks came in, and on the memo line of the checks was written, "For shelving."

"Hey! Denny, we now have $240 to buy shelving."

We drove up to a local Home Depot and looked at what they offered. Denny said it would cost $298 to buy the amount of shelving needed to store all the frames.

"We only have $240," I said.

"I donated $100 to God's Eyes a week ago, so just take the difference out of that."

"Well, Denny, when you gave me the $100 you never said it was for shelving. Besides, I believe that if God wanted us to have $58 more for shelving, he would have sent us $298 and not $240."

Denny knew that if we didn't buy $298 of shelving we wouldn't have enough shelving for everything. He probably thought I was an idiot at the time; however, he once again agreed to go along with what I said.

When we asked that Home Depot employee to get us $240 worth of shelving, he said they didn't have that many units in stock but their store in the next town over had it in inventory. We headed over there and, on the way, we passed a Sam's Club. I told Denny we should stop there and check out their shelving offers. Their shelving was much nicer and was one foot wider, deeper, and one foot taller than Home Depot's shelving. Denny calculated it all out and said that the larger Sam's Club shelving would give us enough room for all the frames to fit.

When we checked out, the total came to $239.92. Denny smiled and was bug-eyed. Immediately we both relearned that God provided for what we needed. God had only sent us $240 because that was all we needed.

It was funny to me how the Creator of the universe wasn't a very good accountant. He was off by eight cents. I pondered giving it to Denny as a reward for his patience and faith, but since he'd just donate it back to God's Eyes, I kept the change and just put it in our petty cash fund.

Denny had just witnessed what he was hoping to see - Father at work. He was amazed by how Father provided exactly the amount we needed, and he relearned that praying and waiting on the Lord was always the right thing to do!

Chapter Fourteen
TIME TO GROW UP

There's a verse in the book of Ephesians, that says *"We are to grow up into Him, which is the head, into Christ."* (EPH 4:15)

I guess "to grow up" is probably the goal or should be the goal of most devoted followers of Christ. After spending the first few years fumbling through the day-to-day operations of running God's Eyes full-time without a clue of how to do that, I guess I too, finally began to grow up a bit spiritually.

I started out being such a reluctant missionary, but as time passed some of my original reluctance diminished and slowly began to be replaced with stronger faith. Along the way, Jenn and I began to develop a deep intimacy with Father. We discovered that to be the most wonderful and valuable thing we have ever acquired.

Over fifteen years have come and gone since I first started this journey and I've now been on over 100 eye and medical mission trips. Despite my complete lack of any prerequisites to become a missionary, God's Eyes has continued to grow. I suppose Father just uses a *willing* heart.

As my heart became willing my desires and hopes changed. One of my greatest desires now, is that all those I encounter will be able to see clearly and that they shall see God.

The next part of the book is devoted to some of the hundreds of stories and lessons, in no particular order, that I've learned and experienced along this journey into obedience. Some are humorous and perhaps some are heartbreaking, but I hope the sum total of all of them will in some way be uplifting to you. And that they will help you to grow up into Christ and cause your faith to grow deeper and stronger.

Chapter Fifteen

THAT'S NOT NECESSARY

A friend, Doug Barclay, invited me to visit him where he worked at the headquarters of Operation Mobilization. It was an organization I had vaguely heard about. Surprisingly, it was quietly tucked away outside the small town of Tyrone, less than fifteen miles from my home.

Operation Mobilization is a large, worldwide ministry that oversees about 6,800 missionaries all over the world. They operate in over 1,100 ports in approximately 140 nations. They have a few large cruise ships known for their "floating libraries" where visitors can select from thousands of books. Each boat has been converted into centers dedicated to constructing orphanages, building shelters for victims of natural disasters, and distributing medical aid, food, and supplies. As they do this, they also share the message of Jesus and His love.

Doug told me he had set up a meeting with Dr. Pat Riley. Pat was head over all of the medical missions and oversaw all their short-term medical trips.

Jenn and I decided to be well prepared for the meeting. We put together a package to promote our ministry that included a PowerPoint presentation for him to review. However, after meeting with him for just a few minutes, he stopped me from talking.

"I've heard enough. I want you to come on all of the medical short-term trips we do," he said.

I didn't even get to play the PowerPoint presentation we had spent so much time and effort making.

"Would you like to see our PowerPoint presentation?" I asked.

"No. If you can do what you just told me you've been doing, that's all I need to hear." Then he left.

All those hours spent putting together a PowerPoint presentation was unnecessary and never needed at all. What a complete waste of our time and effort that was.

Before he left, he handed me a piece of paper with someone's phone number on it, he explained.

"Someone just gave me this guy's phone number, and he left a message saying something along the lines that he has eyeglasses to donate. I think I got this message by mistake. Perhaps I received this so I could give it to you."

After the surprisingly brief meeting, I went home, and I called the number on the slip of paper he had given me.

I conveyed to the man how I had received his number and explained I understood he had some eyeglass supplies he wanted to donate.

"Nope, I don't have any eyeglasses to donate. I have owned optical stores in the past, but now I'm a missionary. My parents were missionaries in Africa, and I was raised there. Now I'm trying to raise support so that I can get back there, to my home country," he explained.

"There must have been some kind of mix-up," I apologized.

Then he invited me to meet with him sometime. He said he would love to hear more about God's Eyes. We set up a time to meet two weeks later at a Starbucks for a chat and some coffee..

As the time to meet approached, I thought I shouldn't even waste my time going because I thought the conversation would eventually get to the place where he would ask me to support him and I had no additional funds to be able to do that. When the day came, I decided that I would at least show up.

He asked me to tell him about God's Eyes and I did. When I was finished, he had tears running down his face. He wiped them from his eyes and spoke.

"Pat Robertson from the 700 Club needs to hear about you." Then he pulled out his phone and made a phone call.

"Hello, Barbara, it's Al, I need to talk with Pat. Oh? He won't be back until Tuesday? Tell him I called and have him call me back."

"You know Pat Robertson?" I was dumbfounded.

"Yes," he replied and then he told me a story about how his grandfather started a mission and had moved to the Congo in Africa where he spent the rest of his life.

"My parents took over that ministry and I was born there and grew up in the Congo. I speak nine different African dialects and I'm Pat Robertson's translator. He takes me with him whenever he goes to Africa. I fly on his private jet with him. I'll set up a meeting with you and him after he calls me back."

"Well, I'm leaving for Haiti next week … to visit the clinic where I send glasses," I told him.

"No problem. By the time you're back, I'll have the meeting arranged."

Wow! Was I ever glad I went to have coffee with him!

I left for Haiti and when I returned, the following voicemail was on my phone.

"Hi, Bryan, this is Al. You meet with Pat on March 13th at 11 a.m. at his office in Virginia Beach, Virginia."

That's crazy, I thought. I'm just starting out as a missionary, I've only been on a few trips and now I'm going to meet with Pat Robertson, one of the biggest names in modern Christian circles. Unbelievable. Why is he even meeting with me?

Once again Jenn and I went to work and created a portfolio for God's Eyes. In it, I detailed my nineteen-page business plan as to how I would accomplish what I thought God wanted me to do through God's Eyes. We even made another DVD showing what we did on the few trips I had taken. We put it all together in a professional-looking leather-wrapped binder. "Surely this will impress Pat," I thought.

On March 13 I drove eight hours to Virginia for my meeting with Pat. When I walked into his reception area, Barbara, his secretary, told me to have a seat and that Pat would see me shortly. I was shaking with excitement. I still had no idea why a man, with one of the largest Christian ministries in the country, would want to spend his valuable time speaking to an unknown guy from a newly emerging little Mom-and-Pop ministry.

"You can go in now. You have 15 minutes." As Barbara was speaking, my phone rang. It was my son.

"Well, how did it go, Dad?" my son inquired.

"I'm on my way in right now. Pray for me, I'm nervous," I whispered.

"Why would you be nervous, Dad? The same Holy Spirit that lives in your heart lives in Pat's. He's got this. It's all a done deal."

"Pray for me, anyway!"

I went in to see Pat carrying the leather-bound portfolio containing my business plan, photos, and our non-professionally made DVD.

Pat introduced himself and we sat down. I began to talk, but I didn't know what to say. I knew my time was short, so I just started rattling on about how Father called me into the ministry and what had happened on my trips. I also mentioned my plans for the ministry. We conversed back and forth a bit more.

"Bryan, this sounds like a worthy ministry. I want to contribute to it personally."

I handed him the portfolio, which he fanned through for all of five seconds and then he handed it back.

"I don't need this," he said, shaking his head from side to side.

"Should I leave it with Barbara?"

"Nope, that's not necessary."

We continued to talk some more. Forget about the fifteen minutes, Pat spoke with me for an hour and ten minutes. Before I left his office Pat told me three different times that God's Eyes was a "worthy ministry." He reiterated that he would send me a personal check and pray for me. Then he sent me on my way with a prayer and his blessing.

I guess my son was right again. It was a done deal before I ever stepped into his office. All those many hours spent writing my business plans and making a pseudo-professional-looking DVD were for naught. It was just like Pat said, "Not necessary."

I should have learned all this the first time after Dr. Pat Riley from Operation Mobilization didn't need to see my PowerPoint presentation either. I vowed to myself to never make another DVD or PowerPoint presentation if the person I was seeing had the first name of Pat.

On the long drive home, I asked Father why Pat didn't even read my business plan. After all, Jen and I spent a long time preparing it.

Father spoke to me:

"Listen to me, Bryan, I got this. God's Eyes is my ministry, not yours. I have plans for God's Eyes. I'm not interested in yours."

I was still learning. I was learning to let God get things done and not interfere. He doesn't need my ideas or input. I was learning to be free from the need to impress people with fancy-looking plans and video presentations. If I would only remember this teaching it would save me a lot of needless effort and waste of time.

Isaiah 55:8 says:
"My ways are not your ways. Neither are my thoughts your thoughts."

A FEW WEEKS LATER I RECEIVED AN ENVELOPE FROM Pat. He had kept his word. It contained a letter of encouragement and a personal check from Pat to God's Eyes for $10,000. I still have that letter today framed on the wall by my desk at God's Eyes. What Pat never knew was that money helped us buy some desperately needed testing equipment and the lenses necessary to build our first complete eye kit. We used that kit to give the next thousand people we helped, the gift of sight.

Here's what Pat wrote to me:

Dear Bryan,
I appreciate the work you and Al are doing through God's Eyes to bring sight to the blind.

I hope the enclosed contribution will help your ministry, and that it will be a great blessing to those who would otherwise remain in darkness—physically and spiritually.

May God continue to bless you is my prayer. I am

Sincerely,
Pat Robertson

*Rick Smith and me standing with a mountain villager
who received new eyeglasses.*

*A little boy asked me for a bible who I found
reading it later at the well in his village.*

Chapter Sixteen
JUST ASK ME

After my first trip to Haiti, life slowly settled back to its normal routine. Throughout the day I kept trying to push thoughts of giving eyeglasses to poor people to the back of my mind, but those thoughts just kept creeping back in.

I eventually started to ponder how I could help fill those frame boards in that Haitian clinic. I could buy frames wholesale, and for $20,000 the entire optical shop would be filled with relatively good quality frames. I didn't have that much money anymore, but I began to think that it wasn't a lot of money to raise. I knew thousands of patients from decades of working in the optical field, and I had a lot of friends as well. I knew if I called them enough times, they would each send me something just to keep me from calling them again. It might take four or five calls, but if I pestered them enough, I could make it happen.

"Besides," I thought, "This was for a good cause. They should do it anyway. They could send the money to God's Eyes and then get a tax break for it."

It would be so simple.

But then I remembered how the biography of George Mueller had moved me. God had provided for him to care for thousands of orphans without ever asking people for money. It was a model of trusting God to which I had committed many months before.

I was certain I needed to learn to trust in God alone to provide and not rely on my efforts. So, that night I said a prayer that went something like this:

"Father, if you want to use me to fill up that optical shop, I'm willing. So, if that's what you want, then send me 500 frames and I will get them to Haiti. In fact, send me more than that because we're going to give those 500 frames away rather quickly and we'll need to refill the frame displays."

Two days later I received an email.

"Hello, Bryan, my name is Frank. I met you at Vision Expo West."

Vision Expo West was a large eye convention I had attended seven months prior, and Frank was the president of a frame company. He continued:

"I have learned of your charitable group and I'm going to send you 100,000 new frames."

I remember reading that aloud to my wife and the first time I read it, I thought it said only 10,000 frames.

"WHAT ?!!" she shouted.

Then I reread it.

"Oops! It's not 10,000. It's a HUNDRED THOUSAND!"

Many eye doctors will never sell 100,000 frames during their entire careers. One hundred thousand frames was a tremendous amount and would have a retail value in the millions of dollars.

MAYBE GOD WOULD HAVE ALLOWED ME TO FILL THAT Haitian optical center the way I originally thought. I was going to ask everyone I knew to send me money. but I learned that God's *A* plan is always this:

"Just ask me!"

Ephesians 3:20 teaches:

"He can do more than we can ask for or imagine."

THAT VERSE IS TRUE AND THAT'S EXACTLY WHAT God can do. More than we can imagine! These 100,000 frames were far more than I had ever imagined. If I had used my efforts to raise funds to purchase frames, I might have been successful for a while, but I would have been tempted to say that I made it happen. There's no glory for God in that. Plus, I would have limited Him.

That night after experiencing how Father had answered my prayer, I told God I would never ask people for money.

There is a huge difference between working for God and allowing God to work through you. It's all about surrendering. We don't need to do God's work by taking things into our own hands. Instead, we need to put ourselves into His hands trustingly and see what happens. Abiding in Him comes first.

I have a strong belief that if Father wants a ministry to exist then He will fund it. He will provide exactly as much as I need to do what He wants me to do. Not more and not less. I was discovering that when I am aligned with His purposes, God supplies the needed resources.

I believe he always wanted me to just pray about resources, anyway.

My personal resources were wilting, but God's were just beginning to be released.

Chapter Seventeen

WHO HUNG LIGHTS IN THE SKY?

Most of the time when we hold free God's Eyes clinics, very large crowds show up. Some days hundreds and other days over a thousand people show up. It doesn't matter how large our eye teams are, we would never be able to help 1000 people a day. It can also cause problems as people sometimes get tired of waiting and begin to push and shove to be the next one helped. They are desperate for sight, and we are their hope. They need our help, but we don't always get to help everyone. At one clinic I saw an eighty year old woman punch one of our men in the face when he told her she would have to come back on the following day. I've had to get used to the horrible feeling I get when we leave a village and there are people left over who waited for many hours but were never helped.

One of the times, when more people showed up than we could help, was in Nicaragua. We handed out tickets with numbers and told everyone else who didn't get a number to come back another day.

Late in the afternoon, a mother came in with her nine-year-old son. They had left home early that day and had walked for hours to get to where our clinic was being held. She informed me that they had only been given one number, but both needed to be tested and asked if I would please help both of them. She was probably the twentieth person to ask me that same thing that day. I looked outside at the long line of people left and I told her I was extremely sorry, but I could only help one of them due to the large number of people who still needed to be seen. She told me to help her son as he could hardly see anything at all. I tested his eyes, and she was right. He was extremely nearsighted and desperately needed very high-powered lenses to see clearly. He needed more power than anyone I had tested that day. When I was finished, I sent them to the table where the glasses were assembled. I continued to see more patients. That little guy saw his mom clearly for the first time in his life that day.

The following day was like the first, more people than we could help showed up. The same lady, whose little boy got glasses the day before, had made the long walk back to get herself a pair. She somehow ended up back in my line and I recognized her when it was her turn. I told her how sorry I was that I couldn't help her the day before and I was very glad she was able to return.

"How is your little boy doing with his new glasses?" I asked.

"He loves them." Last night he asked me, "Who hung lights in the sky?"

I was dumbfounded. Did he say, "Who hung lights in the sky?" Had this little guy never seen a star before? The thought of that blew me away. This young boy had just seen something he never knew existed and he didn't even know what it was called. It was one of those moments when I realized the powerful effect eyeglasses can have on someone. It must have been a magnificent moment for him when he saw those stars for the first time and experienced the awesome beauty of God's star-covered sky.

Three times in my life my breath has been taken away when I gazed upon the night sky as it was illuminated by billions of stars. It once happened in the bushlands of Zambia, once while I was in the prairie in central South Dakota, and once on the island of Haiti.

I don't remember what the sky looked like the night that little guy first saw a star, but I'm positive Father put on a dazzling display for him … one that he would never forget. I realized that that special moment occurred all because of a simple act of kindness. When we offer up the gifts and resources that we possess, we become the givers of those moments.

Another time we were working over 10,000 feet up in the Andes Mountains in Peru. We worked at night in a very small church lit up by a single lightbulb. An 83-year-old man came hoping he could read again. He told me he hadn't read his Bible for over thirty years since he could no longer make out what the words said. It was cold up on the mountain where he lived year-round, so he always wore a jacket, and he kept a small Bible in the chest pocket of his jacket. Even though he could no longer read the words of God, he wanted them to be near to his heart.

I tested his eyes. He needed enormously powerful lenses if he was to ever read again. As I was assembling them, he took his Bible out of his coat pocket and held it in his hands in anticipation of being able to read once again. When I returned, he was standing there with his Bible held in front of his face. He had waited for years for that moment to occur. When I placed the glasses on this tiny old man, he read a Bible verse for the first time in decades. He began to weep because he could see to read again. Immediately he started to enjoy reading the words in the book that God had written especially for him.

AT ONE OF OUR PANAMA CLINICS, A MIDDLE-AGED woman came in to be tested. She, like so many others we help, was very nearsighted and very poor. She had never been to an eye doctor in her life, so she had never owned eyeglasses. Her eyesight was unbelievably bad. When I placed the new glasses on her, she lit up. She was elated and started telling me everything she could see. Then she started running around the church declaring to everyone how she could see, and when she looked outside, she was ecstatic.

"Leaves, oh my! I can see the leaves on the trees!"

For forty-five minutes I heard her in the background as she ran around that church describing each and everything she saw. Her overpowering joy caused her to jump animatedly up and down. Her excitement brought joy to my own heart.

IN A VILLAGE NEAR THE OCEAN ON THE WEST COAST of Ecuador, a man went for a walk. He told me he didn't know there was a free eye clinic being held that day until he walked by. After accidentally stumbling upon us, he waited in line for a long time. He, like so many others, had never seen clearly before. He was overwhelmed when we placed his first pair of eyeglasses on his head. He came back to my testing area after getting his new glasses and told me the following story.

He said that very night his daughter was going to graduate from high school. She would be the first member in the history of his family to ever do that. He told me he had planned on going to the ceremony that evening to hear his daughter graduate, but instead of just hearing, he was now going to be able to see his daughter graduate! He thanked me profusely for his new clear sight!

This is what God's Eyes does. We travel to some of the poorest places on the planet to help little nine-year-old boys see stars in the sky at night and help 83-year-old men read the loving words of God again. We cause middle-aged women to dance around churches shouting about what they can see and we help dads see their daughters graduate from high school. We help them and many more by offering the incredible gift called sight.

I was invited to speak at a church one day. The pastor began interviewing me in front of the congregation.

"Why do you do what you do, Bryan?"

I paused for a moment then replied, "Well, sometimes I get to be with a person at the very moment that they see clearly for the first time in their life. There are just no words to describe the wonder and joy of those moments. And sometimes I even get to be with a person the moment they receive the gift of eternal life. Those times are even more wonderful than the former. You ask me why I do what I do? I would have to answer you, "Why wouldn't I do what I do?

Chapter Eighteen
A PUNCH IN THE FACE

I'VE TRAVELED TO HONDURAS ON SEVERAL DIFFER-
ent occasions, and sometimes I go to places that only a few have ever heard
of. One village didn't even have a "village." It was just a clearing in the woods
where locals raised three tarps and put them on branches that hung from
trees to give some sort of shelter from the sun. To get there we drove on paved
roads, then for some time on dirt roads, and finally for a long time on what
I call goat trails with ankle-deep ruts in the dirt. When we couldn't drive the
bus any farther, we stopped and unloaded the supplies. Then we carried the
supplies from the bus down a dirt trail for about a half-mile.

When we first arrived about 150 people were waiting for us. By the end
of the day, we saw more than twice that many. People just kept appearing
from seemingly nowhere in the woods. Many people prayed to receive Christ
that day. It was a hot day and once again the people were so thankful that we
had visited them.

These non-picture-perfect types of places are where I enjoy holding eye
clinics the most. We taped the eye charts onto the side of a truck because there
were no buildings anywhere. The bathroom was a hole in the ground enclosed
by a few pieces of plastic bags tied to branches for privacy. We helped many
people see that day including a lady who needed forty steps of power in each
eye to see clearly. That is a very high prescription. She was another one of those

people who saw objects clearly for the first time in her life. There was also a small boy who was extremely nearsighted. The new eyeglasses we made him will certainly change his life forever!

The next day was our hardest one. We were in a school in a town like any poor small town in the States. We set up the eye clinic in a classroom where it was well over 90 degrees.

What made it such a difficult day was not the heat, but rather the fact that some teachers, the principal, and other local authorities brought friends to the clinic throughout the day. They demanded they be helped first, even though many locals had been waiting in line in the hot sun for hours. It almost came to fistfights between the haves and have-nots.

Many times, that day, after we finished with a patient and they got up to leave, there would be a mad dash for the empty exam chair. Those in authority told us we had to kick the poor person out of the chair and wait on their friends instead.

All these affluent people were demanding, and some were downright greedy and mean. They often abused their position of power to secure handfuls of supplies for as many people as they wanted. I hate being forced to partake in this type of injustice. This was one of the few times I ever saw my wife, Jennifer become frustrated with what was going on. Thankfully this didn't occur anywhere else on that trip.

The rest of that trip was wonderful. Every day we would travel to a very poor village in some crazy out-of-the-way location. Just getting there was an adventure. Several times we had to carry all the equipment up or down muddy roads because the bus or the trucks couldn't make it through the rough terrain. Several times it rained on us, but that was fine because it would help cool things off.

Every place we went hundreds of people showed up to be helped. By the third day, someone said over a hundred people had prayed to receive Christ as Lord. After that, no one even kept count, but I would guess by the end of the trip more than twice that many had done the same.

The poor are almost always so gracious and thankful. However, in one little village, this took place:

As we walked up to the little school that we would be working in, many of the children came running up to us. I think they had learned that missionaries mean toys, candies, and soccer balls. The children leaped into the arms of our team members, and I knelt to reach for a boy who may have been around eleven- or twelve years old who was running towards me. As I reached out to lift him and hug him, he reached his arm back and punched me in the face as hard as he could, and then he ran away. I couldn't believe it. I came here to help him and to love on him and he punched me hard. What a nice welcome, I thought. Thank God no one else has ever greeted me the same way.

Sometimes you get so exhausted while working in this type of poverty day after day, but after you help someone see and they hug you or kiss you or just smile back at you it's enough to keep you going

The work we do is most certainly tiring and occasionally the conditions almost border on ridiculous, but God offers us joy anyway. We are servants of the Lord to the poor, sent to open their eyes and share the love of Jesus. I wish I could better explain the wonders that God has allowed Jenn and me to have while serving Him. His love, though, is indescribable so I guess I will just leave it at that.

Chapter Nineteen

AN EARLY YEAR IN RETROSPECT

Early on in God's Eyes, I wrote down some of my memories of the previous year. Here are those reflections:

LAST YEAR I HELD A SICK BABY IN MY ARMS. HE HAD no parents and had no hope. God loves this baby boy, so He asked some people to care for him. They said yes to serving God and because they did this little guy lived. Then I saw a mother who was forced by her poverty to watch her baby boy starve to death. She was too poor to help him. She had five other children at home and there was just no money. Her poverty forced her into a terrible situation. She had to make the impossible choice of which of her children got fed, and which one would die.

I asked God why he planned for that to happen. He said he didn't. He said he asked someone to send money to feed the baby and they said no. He asked someone to provide clothes for the baby, and they didn't. He asked people to donate medicine so that babies like him don't get sick, and they said no. And He asked someone to go and adopt him. They didn't. God loved this baby. He had plans for this baby not to be harmed. But the people God asked all said no or did nothing. When we say no to what God asks us to do, a baby may die somewhere as this one did.

LAST YEAR GOD INTRODUCED ME TO A YOUNG LADY
in her late twenties. God asked her to leap from the comforts of the States to
a dangerous area in Haiti. She is a nurse. Every day she works long hours in
very hard conditions, and she is constantly stretched to her limits. Hundreds of
people are alive today because she said yes to God. Her stories are of constant
encouragement to me.

LAST YEAR I MET AN EYE SURGEON, WHO TRAVELS
to a town 8 hours away, several times a month to help others see. God loves
the people in the little town she travels to, and He is concerned about their
lack of sight. He asked her to go and help them. She receives no pay for her
labor, and it makes her life busier and more complicated. But she said yes to
God and a thousand extra people a year get to see clearly because of her.

LAST YEAR GOD ALLOWED ME TO MEET A DENTIST
who lives a very simple existence in a very poor place. Within a few hours of
her house, there were numerous little mountain villages where even poorer
people live. Thirty years ago, God asked her to serve Him. So she gave up her
plans for comfort and abundance. She started leading groups of visiting medical
teams into these villages to bring care to people God loves. Thousands of people
have been comforted and can still smile because she accepted this challenge.

LAST YEAR GOD HAD ME TRAVEL WITH A PASTOR IN
Haiti whose life is threatened daily. He had to send his family far away to live
in another country for fear that they would be kidnapped. He is no longer able
to enjoy daily life with them … instead, he serves God by building schools,
churches, and medical clinics in places where there are none. He has taken a
leap of faith and I'm astonished by what he has accomplished.

LAST YEAR I MET A HUNDRED MORE PEOPLE WHO
said yes when God asked them to help others. Some of those people live here
in the States and some have moved far, far away to distant countries. All of

them have become the best people I have ever met. They all share the heart and love of God, and they exhibit the fruit of the Spirit. They have all taken a leap of faith and that has taken some of them to places they never knew existed. Thousands of needy people are comforted because of their obedience.

LAST YEAR I PUT GLASSES ON A NINETY-YEAR-OLD man who walked for four hours to see me. I put glasses on a three-year-old girl who needed 100 steps of power to see clearly, and I put glasses on thousands of other people in between. I fitted glasses by candlelight when there was no electricity, and I gave eyeglasses to people while working in a church with no roof and only mud for a floor.

LAST YEAR GOD ASKED ME TO TRAVEL TO SOME OF the poorest places on earth where I put eyeglasses on the people who He loves and cares for even though many of them have no idea who He is. I laughed with them, cried, rejoiced, smiled, and prayed with these people who God cares so much about that He sent help to so they could see again.

LAST YEAR, HOWEVER, I ALSO SAW PEOPLE WHO WENT blind because they did not receive the help they needed. I saw people die from starvation and saw people who ate mud because they had no food. I saw children suffering from typhoid and all sorts of curable diseases and heard them crying in pain at night because they did not have the medicine they needed to comfort them. I saw illiterate unemployed people who never got the chance to learn or go to a school whose lives were slowly wasting away in sheer boredom. I saw people born in such isolated places they would never have hope of ever finding work. Some drowned in floods and others lost their crops to droughts. I saw multitudes of people hurting in every way possible from the injustices that extreme poverty produces.

BRYAN KAISER

LAST YEAR I SAW A LOT OF NEEDLESS SUFFERING ...
lots and lots of needless suffering. Because somewhere, someone said NO when
they were asked to do something.

LAST YEAR INSTEAD OF WORKING NEAR HOME IN A
beautiful upscale eye practice, where everyone and everything is beautiful,
I worked far away in third world countries in some extremely hot and dry
conditions. I worked during monsoons, where the rain soaked us to the bone
and made the trip back to our base almost impossible. I went to sleep in places
where I never could have imagined staying. I went to places where my life was
threatened, and I had to be protected at night by men with guns and machetes.
I've eaten things I don't ever want to taste again. I've been sick in the field
with stomach viruses and suffered from diarrhea in places where there were
no bathrooms. I even acquired parasites. I traveled up roadless mountains and
through deserts where we got flat tires. I carried equipment through fields of
mud and saw people robbed and thousands who were hurting.

LAST YEAR I DID ALL THIS BECAUSE GOD LOVES PEO-
ple, and He asked me to help them see clearly. So, I left the life I knew and
said yes to a journey that lay unknown before me. Last year with the help you
all gave me, I was able to help thousands of people see and I saw hundreds of
people discover who God is. Last year ... I learned to leap and ... I learned
how others suffer when you don't.

Chapter Twenty
THE JOY OF KIDNEY STONES

One evening while in Uganda I developed a severe stabbing pain starting in my lower back sometime around midnight. I was all too familiar with that pain. It was a kidney stone. I knocked on the room next to mine and asked my friend Dave to find me some pain pills. I was certain that some of the girls on the trip must have something that would help alleviate my pain. I hoped they had brought medication for something like migraines or cramps or hopefully something much stronger. As I lay back down on my bed the pain rapidly grew more intense. This would be the fifth time I had a kidney stone. I knew just how intense the pain would become.

I also knew that every other time I had had a stone I went to the hospital where a CAT scan was performed to determine whether the stone was small enough to pass. That was not going to be possible here. The nearest place to have that done would have required an eight-hour drive via dirt, pothole-filled roads. I knew I couldn't endure that.

A minister once told me, "A call to ministry is a call to suffering." It was taking on a different meaning for me that day. Sometimes we face trials not because of what we're doing wrong, but because of what we're doing right. I was doing the right thing by being in Uganda helping the poor see. However, I could have been enduring this kidney stone at home in a much more comfortable setting with the help of strong narcotics.

Dave came back a few minutes later and told me all they could muster up was three Advil pills.

"I can't do a kidney stone on three Advil pills!" I exclaimed as I was on the verge of tears.

I wanted morphine! Lots of it. I would have taken heroin or anything at all that would dull the pain. I thought that surely in this dangerous little town there must be some drug dealers.

"Someone please go buy me some illegal drugs," I wished silently.

While lying there in pain I began to think about how the poor must frequently go through similar trials. They have no hospitals to run to when they hurt. They just must suffer in their pain. That's unfortunately the reality for much of the world. They must endure pain at levels and for lengths of time that most of us will fortunately never know. Often there is no hope that the pain will ever be alleviated. The poor are so much tougher than we are. I braced myself that night because I was about to enter that part of their world.

Melanie, Dave, and some of the other people on our team came in to check on me from time to time throughout the night as I squirmed like a worm does when you stick a hook in its back. I put my pillow over my mouth to muffle my screams in hopes of not keeping anyone awake. There was nothing I could do but endure the pain until it ended. Seven hours later the stone passed, and the pain disappeared.

Psalm 30:5 says: *"There will be pain (weeping) in the night, but joy comes in the morning."* That was certainly true for me that day.

THE NEXT MORNING, WE DIDN'T MISS A BEAT, AS WE drove the hour-and-a-half bumpy drive back to Adachar. This time, however, I rode in the front seat of the bus with a pillow wrapped around my sore lower back praying that all those dang potholes wouldn't shake any more kidney stones loose.

Later that day I was talking with one of the guys on the trip who was a self-professed atheist.

"I prayed for you last night," he said.

"Wow! Thank you so much for doing that!"

I paused thinking to myself about how God can work all things, even kidney stones, together for good. Like motivating an atheist to pray.

"Who did you pray to?" I asked him.

"To God."

"I thought you didn't believe in God."

"What I don't believe in is eternity. Nothing is eternal, everything has a life cycle. This life is all we have."

After that, we had many talks together throughout the rest of that trip and by the end of it, I mentioned that 1,200 people belonged to the church that I attended.

"I would pick you to be on my team before 1,100 of those church members," I told him. He was a humanitarian spending his life being kind to others. He lived his life with deeper and more loving convictions than most of the Christians I knew.

My final encouragement to him was that eternity was a lot closer than he thought. It was only a decision away.

Chapter Twenty-One
HOW DID THAT HAPPEN?

Two years into my ministry I had partnered up with a friend, Tim, who I knew previously from my church. Early in his career, he was a pastor. After that, he ran a successful business as a financial counselor and divorce mediator. Eventually, he had a desire to return to the ministry again as a pastor, but this time in the country of Panama. There he headed up the only English-speaking church in one of Panama's expatriate communities. The church he ran immediately embraced the work God's Eyes was doing. We partnered together and held eye clinics in various parts of Panama.

On my third trip there, I brought down a small team of volunteers from the States. We worked long days helping as many people as we could. It was here that I began the idea of establishing prayer teams. We would be able to not only help with eye care needs but with spiritual needs as well. His church was filled with many comfortably retired people who eagerly volunteered at every clinic.

Every day on that trip we saw more people than I had planned to help and during the second-to-the-last night we were there, I realized we were short on supplies. I counted how many frames we had remaining in our eye kits for our final day of clinics. We only had twenty-seven frames left with which we could make prescription eyeglasses. I knew that wouldn't be enough. I figured that once we ran out of frames I could take the unfilled orders back home, assemble the glasses and ship them back to Tim's church. However, I was counting on members from Tim's church to drive back to the village and distribute those glasses.

The next day it was once again ridiculously hot in the church where we were working. On top of that, the room I worked in was full of thousands of little fleas. I must have been a delicacy to them because they enjoyed feasting on my ankles and calves all day long. The army of fleas was alarmingly abundant, and we had no bug spray. I did, however, find a can of insecticide in the church bathroom. I was eager to be bug-free so throughout the day I drenched my legs with this can of Raid Ant and Roach Killer every hour or so to try to stop the biting. I was miserable, but I survived the heat and the bites that day.

When we finally finished all the patients we had planned to help that day, I was ecstatic that we had completed another God's Eyes mission. Then some of the people at the church asked if we could help the pastor and his family.

"Oh, how many is that?" I inquired unenthusiastically.

"Five."

Well, of course, we had to help them. How could we say no to the pastor and his family? We continued working. Then as happens in so many of our clinics, a family arrived that had just walked eight hours to get there and asked if we would please help them. How can you turn someone like that away? Next, we were informed that some police officers arrived and that some nurses were on the way, and they requested that we stay and help them as well. Then another person who had a sad story and another and another and another. This continued for hours.

Finally, they told me if I would just see one more patient, they promised they would send everyone else home. It was about the tenth time they made that promise to me, so I no longer believed anything they said. I was frustrated, but I agreed to see one more. I hate turning people away but sometimes you just can't fight the fatigue any longer.

"This will be the last one, I mean that, and then I'm walking out!"

They sent a lady in, and she turned out to be the eighty-seventh person I helped that day. I refracted her eyes and she desperately needed extremely high-powered lenses to be able to read. I asked my friends about our supplies.

"How many frames do we have left?" I asked Joe who had assembled all our glasses that day.

"We just have one frame left in the box."

I told him the powers of lenses he needed to put into the frame.

I then turned back to the lady I was helping.

"I have to tell you something. You are incredibly lucky that you're getting glasses today because we started the day with only enough frames to make twenty-seven pairs of glasses. I have no idea how we possibly have any frames left to make your glasses with, but somehow, we have one left. So, you will be getting the glasses you need!"

She spoke English well.

"Well, let me tell you a story. I am a pastor at another church. When I learned that you were all going to be here, I planned on coming because my only pair of reading glasses broke a long time ago. I don't have enough money to buy a new pair. It's been very challenging to be a pastor and not be able to read my Bible. So today I arrived here very early … way before you ever got here. I asked if I could be added to the list of patients to be seen and they told me that I could not. They said you had told them you could only help fifty people today and that they already had seventy-two people on the list. I asked them if they would mind if I waited anyway. They said I was welcome to wait all day if I wanted to, but that I wouldn't be helped. Well, the Lord told me differently. Early this morning He said that if I would be patient, He would make sure I would get new glasses. So you see, I knew that if I waited that's exactly what would happen; I was going to get glasses. So I've waited here for eleven hours."

Wow, what faith she had! She knew with certainty that if she waited on the Lord, He would provide what she needed. On the last day of our trip, the last person I refracted got the last pair of eyeglasses we could make. Father once again showed up in His perfect timing.

Later I talked to my friend Joe, who oversaw making all the glasses that day. "Where did you get all the frames from?"

How did we help more people today than we had supplies for? I wondered.

"I don't know how that happened either! But throughout the day I would find a left temple here and then a frame front somewhere else and later a right temple would show up. Throughout the day I just kept putting more frames together from all the parts I kept discovering."

"But we don't bring frame parts," I said. "All of our frames are bought pre-assembled. I've never brought parts of frames on any trip ever."

But somehow Joe just kept finding parts!

Can Father make parts of frames appear at an eye clinic in the middle of a poor village? No, that would be impossible by all our reasoning and logic. To think that possible would be nonsense. Our reasoning cannot explain anything like that.

Ecclesiastes 8: 17 says, *I saw that no one can understand all that God does. People can try and try to understand the things that happen here on earth, but they cannot.*

I GUESS IF FATHER CAN MAKE AN ENTIRE UNIVERSE, then He must be able to make frame parts appear.

I was beginning to give up on trying to understand all that was happening at God's Eyes events and slowly quit questioning God's ability to do anything. Especially simple things like making frame parts appear at an eye clinic that is helping the poor to see. Instead of doubting things I couldn't explain I was beginning to anticipate them.

It says this in 1 Corinthians 2:14:

"The natural person does not accept the things of the Spirit of God, for they are folly to him, and he is not able to understand them because they can only be spiritually discerned."

Once while in Zambia I asked a well-educated, intelligent man from India who became a missionary to Africa, whether he had ever experienced something he could not explain while serving in Africa? I'll never forget his answer:

"Yes, I have seen many strange things happen that do not align with my theology."

After a few years of being in the field, I knew exactly what he meant. My limited theology and understanding are unable to explain everything I've seen.

Chapter Twenty-Two

MIRACLE IN THE CLOSET

Toward the end of 2014, I returned once again to Haiti. Eight of us from my home church traveled to the small village of Peredo. Here, Pastor RoRo, whom I met five years before, had finished building a small medical clinic in this out-of-the-way jungle area in the southwest part of the country. We were the first team to ever hold an eye clinic there or any type of clinic.

During the first hour, on the first day, one of the main pieces of equipment I use to determine a patient's prescription had its circuit board destroyed during an electrical surge. I told the pastor we would have to send most of the people home because we no longer had the equipment we needed to examine patients.

"We have an eye computer machine in the closet," he told me.

I doubted him because we were in this crazy remote heavily vegetated small village where no eye clinic had ever been held before.

We politely quarreled for a few minutes, and finally, I spoke out:

"There is no way that you have the specialized piece of equipment that I need!"

Exasperated, he sent an assistant to the closet anyway.

"Just go get it for him," he said.

When he returned, I couldn't believe it! A portable, battery-operated autorefractor. It was just what I needed. A battery-operated unit was needed since the power in the building kept surging on and off. The only bad thing was it didn't have the specialized batteries needed to power it.

But of course, as "luck" would have it, I just happened to have a fully charged lithium battery in my backpack that was exactly the shape, size, and voltage needed to operate this piece of equipment.

Long before we ever knew we would have this need God did. He provided a spare unit for us in a closet inside this medical clinic in the middle of nowhere in Haiti because He knew we would need it.

As it turns out a church group from back in the States had donated it months before. The Haitian pastor had no idea how to use it or even what it was designed to measure, so he placed it away in a storage closet for safekeeping. He was also kind enough to let us use it for the rest of our trip as we continued holding eye clinics throughout other parts of Haiti. Once again God had shown up in unexpected ways providing exactly what we needed.

Chapter Twenty-Three
LOOKING THE OTHER WAY

I went to Uganda on a trip with a local church group. It took us a long time to get where we were going. We took many plane flights, each one lasting several hours. This was followed by two additional days of driving on highways which eventually turned into bumpy dirt roads.

The leader of this trip was a friend of a friend of mine. She had made the trip to this distant part of the northeast corner of Uganda numerous times before. She told me about a place where many orphaned kids gathered each day on this five-acre piece of land to eat food and get medical care. She thought it would be a great place to do a God's Eyes clinic. I agreed, as probably none of those kids had ever had their eyes tested before.

We had a limited amount of time to spend examining the children. Everyone had to leave the compound by 4 p.m. so they could get back to their villages before nightfall. In this part of Uganda, it was too dangerous to be out at night. I heard stories of how local tribes would descend from the nearby mountains and come into this region of the plains of Adachar. They would loot, rob, rape, and even murder some of the families who lived there. Some of the children there had lost their parents to these murderous gangs of thieves. Several of the young children, some as young as nine years old, became heads of their households caring for their younger siblings because their parents had been murdered.

We had quite an eclectic group of twelve on this trip including believers and nonbelievers and people of all ages from teens to grandparents. I had been on at least fifty trips by then, but for some of the brave volunteers, this was their first mission trip.

On our first night in Uganda, we were awakened in the morning by dozens of monkeys climbing up the walls of our hotel. I affectionately named it "Monkey Inn."

From there we traveled for two more days to a small village named Katakwi where we stayed for the remainder of the trip. It wasn't exactly a hotel. The place had three bedrooms in which the guys stayed, and one large common-area room filled with bunk beds for all the girls. After the trip was over, I was told that guards with automatic weapons had been hired to protect us at night. One of the girls told me she woke up early one morning and planned to go for a walk. One of the guards surprised her and motioned angrily, with his automatic rifle, for her to go back into the building. She immediately agreed.

At lunchtime, we would help feed all the kids. We served them posho, which is white corn flour mixed with water. It turns into a paste that looks something like thin mashed potatoes and it tasted like sticky glue. After serving them, we gladly retreated to our small van to eat the food that we had brought for ourselves, instead of those delicious "glue potatoes."

We parked the van every day in a far corner of the fenced-in five acres. The children were told not to go near our bus because that's where we kept our backpacks, purses, food, and water. They were instructed to stay far away from the vehicle.

One day a little girl, maybe five years old, came over to our bus while we were eating lunch on it. She cupped her hands together and lifted them to her mouth, motioning that she wanted something to drink. At this compound, some of the young teenage boys had been given the authority to make sure everyone obeyed the rules. They carried sticks around three feet long. If someone misbehaved or broke the rules they were "corrected" with these sticks.

One of these teen boys saw the little girl standing by our bus. He yelled at her, and she took off running. She knew she wasn't supposed to be there, but it was extremely hot outside, and she just wanted a drink. He chased her and caught up to her about a hundred yards from the bus. He began to beat her with a stick the thickness of a broom handle. She fell to the ground in a fetal position screaming as she was being hit again and again. I jumped off the bus, ran over to the boy, stopped him from striking her, and then escorted him across the compound over to the head administrator.

"This boy just severely beat that little girl way over there who only wanted a cup of water!" I told him. I pointed to where she was in the distance, still lying in the field, crying.

"I will handle this!" the administrator said in his very deep voice.

He grabbed the teen boy and we all walked back to where the beaten girl was lying.

"Stand up!" the administrator ordered her. She stood up, still crying.

"Apologize to him for making him beat you!"

"No way!" I screamed silently to myself in horror.

This couldn't be happening! How in the world was this her fault? That's how it was in that part of Uganda. Men sometimes beat women and somehow, it's justified.

I didn't want to be in Uganda anymore after that. It's very difficult to observe injustices that are considered acceptable by the inhabitants of a region. In some countries, children get beaten or raped, and the culture in those countries just tends to look the other way. Often the police do nothing at all. A missionary OBGYN doctor once told me she reported to the police that a little girl she examined had been raped. The police came, took the girl away, and then raped her. The doctor said she no longer calls the police anymore.

I don't care to go to countries that turn a blind eye to such abuses, however, I know I must go. I cannot legislate morality, but I can offer my talents to correct vision and do what I'm called to do. It's hard but I know that the Judge of all the Earth will make things right one day. For now, I must humbly do my part. I must bring vision and the good news of Jesus to the world, even in locations where extreme injustice exists.

Chapter Twenty-Four
CRITTERS AND CRAPPY PLACES

When I ask people why they don't come on mission trips the number one answer I get is:

"I don't like bugs and the bathrooms are terrible."

I always imagine this funny scene in my head when I hear that. At the end of their lives when they die, they are standing in front of St. Peter at the Pearly Gates, and he questions them:

"Why didn't you do any mission trips in your lifetime?"

"Well, you know, there would be so many bugs in those countries and the bathrooms in those places are ridiculous!"

"Oh … OK," St. Peter says," Those are great excuses," and he opens the gates and lets them in.

I'm not sure, however, that Father would be that easily convinced. It is true though, that there are often many bugs and, yes, you probably will encounter some lousy bathrooms on our God's Eyes trips. Here are a few funny stories about those conditions. I hope they will only make you laugh and that they do not convince you to never go on a missionary trip.

ONCE WHEN I WAS SERVING IN HONDURAS, WE HELD a clinic in a two-room cinder block school building. There was an outhouse and I was glad to see it. I had been having diarrhea all morning, most likely from something I ate, and the bus ride took a couple of hours to get there. When we arrived, I was more than ready to use the bathroom again. The outhouse was disgusting. An angel of a nurse with our group even volunteered to clean it up for me before I used it, but I shook my head "no." I could no longer wait. It was a kid-sized outhouse, and I was wedged in like a cork in a bottle. My shoulders touched the sides as I sat inside of it. It was that small. It was also pitch dark inside.

None of that mattered to me. I was glad to finally have a bathroom to use. While sitting there emptying my intestines, something furry, about the size and weight of a child's baseball glove, fell onto the top of my head. It began to nestle into my hair and make itself comfortable. Have you ever witnessed a small child fall and get hurt? They don't cry immediately, but they pause for a few seconds as they inhale a large volume of air, then they let out a scream. Well, that's exactly what I did.

I took a deep breath then screamed

"Aaaaaaaaah!"

One of the people on the trip with me was waiting outside for his turn to use the bathroom and he shouted back.

"Are you OK in there?"

"I don't want to be here!" I cried out.

I couldn't jump out of the bathroom as I was in the middle of doing my business, so I leaned forward as far as I could, and I swatted whatever it was that was perched on top of my head. It hit the ground. I never saw what it was because it was too dark. Perhaps it was a frog, a bat, or a large tarantula making his new nest.

There was no ultra-soft Charmin or even banana leaves available, but that didn't matter because as soon as I could I jumped out of that outhouse. I was in such a hurry that I hadn't even pulled my pants up. My ankles were bound, I moved like a penguin as I ran away, then fell to the ground.

IN HAITI ONE TIME, WE WERE OUT FOR A WALK AND the classic Montezuma's revenge hit me yet again. The missionary walking with me who, thank God, could speak Creole, took me up to somebody's shack and asked if I could use their outhouse. As I was sitting in there, I noticed that above my head, in the left-hand corner of the outhouse, was a spider almost as large as my hand. It was by far the largest spider sitting in the largest web I had ever seen. I removed one of my flip-flop sandals, waved it at the eight-legged monster, and threatened him.

"This is my area down here and that is yours up there. If you come into my area, I'm going to have to kill you, so you better not move."

I guess spiders in Haiti understand English, as this one, thank the Lord, never moved the entire time I was there.

DURING AN EYE CLINIC IN GUATEMALA, WE HAD A large team at a school, and we were offering eye care, dental care, and medical care. Next to the school was a row of five outhouses. Every morning the women in that village would honor us by scrubbing down those toilets and cleaning up any messes that were on the ground. They tried their hardest to make the bathrooms less foul-smelling and more pleasant for us. This was one of the humblest acts I had ever witnessed.

Matthew chapter 20:16 says, *"The last shall be first, the first shall be last."*

I'm certain we have no chance of being honored in Heaven before any of these incredibly kind and humble ladies.

IN A SMALL PERUVIAN VILLAGE, I HAD THE SUDDEN need to "go." I asked where their bathrooms were, and they pointed to a spot across the road.

Immediately across the street from where we were working, there was a field about 40-feet wide by 60-feet long enclosed by a three-foot-high stone wall. It was the town "poo" field. If you had to go to the bathroom, you simply peed or squatted and did whatever you had to do right there, right in front of everyone. As I entered this tiny arena of defecation, I realized you had to be careful where you stepped because let's just say, there were deposits from the previous guests all over the place. But when you have to go, you have to go. I had no choice.

I couldn't believe I was about to go to the bathroom outside in public in front of people. "Oh, well, … when in Rome do as the Romans do," I thought.

I squatted down and did my business. I was right there in front of over one hundred people who were waiting to have their eyes examined, as well as anyone else who just happened to walk by. Before I finished, a local elderly man around eighty years old came and joined me. I wasn't certain of the proper poo-field etiquette. It was like being at an Ex-Lax festival! He smiled, nodded, and squatted down just a few feet away from me to do his business, too. I've never pooped outside in public with someone before, in front of an audience, but I did that day.

I have had many first-hand views of the lives of people who are different from me, but this one stole the show.

IN HONDURAS, WE WERE WORKING AT A CHURCH IN an area that didn't even have a name. It was several miles away from the nearest town. The church building consisted of only four walls built out of unpainted masonry blocks and it had no roof. There was no concrete flooring either, only mud.

A pastor, who was on the trip with us, preached while our clinic was being established. By the time he had set up for the sermon, the group of patients had grown from three to about fifteen people. When he stopped preaching there were well over one hundred. They just kept coming, literally from out of the woods. Eventually, many people sat waiting just off the side of the road.

This day was another one of those days when my body just wasn't cooperating with me. I felt ill and foul fluids were coming out of both ends. I looked around and about a hundred feet away in the field behind the church was an outhouse. I quickly scooted over there. I went inside and was bent halfway over clutching my stomach while trying to find the toilet when the pastor's wife walked in. It turned out that it wasn't an outhouse at all. It was the parsonage for the pastor and his wife. They lived in the six-foot-by-six-foot wooden shack I had almost mistakenly chosen to relieve myself in. She looked at me in horror.

"*Donde esta el bano?*" (Where is the bathroom?) I shouted.

"*Bano?*" she asked.

"*Si, si, si,*" I said.

Then she raised her arm and pointed to the left side of the field, then to the center, and finally to the right side of the field, all the while saying,

"*Bano!, Bano!, Bano!*"

In other words, "In the field, you idiot! Not in my house!"

I was never a Boy Scout or a camper so this whole experience of having no toilet and pooping anywhere you wanted to, in an open field, was all new to me. I was squatting down in a wide-open field once again for all the cows and people to see.

I guess it was better than ruining the pastor's living room.

That event prompted me to invent a joke that perhaps only I understand:

"When is an outhouse not an outhouse?"

"When it's somebody's house!"

IN THE SOUTHEAST CORNER OF ECUADOR, WE HELD a clinic in an abandoned government building. Here they had a fancy outhouse. Instead of digging a hole and just placing a shack over the top of it, they had built a five-foot-high concrete staircase. This led up to a concrete platform where a nicely constructed aluminum outhouse was built on top of that base. Once again, I and some of the others on the team were experiencing the joys of diarrhea from something bad we ate.

I walked over to the steps leading up to the outhouse and climbed them and I noticed Gabriel, one of the teenage daughters of the missionaries we were working with. She was sleeping on the top of the stairs. She was too sick with intestinal problems to return to the clinics. After using the facilities, I headed back towards the building where we were holding the eye clinic. After taking only ten steps I had to turn around and run back to use the outhouse again.

Riding in a Cheeva on remote roads I've never heard of in Ecuador.

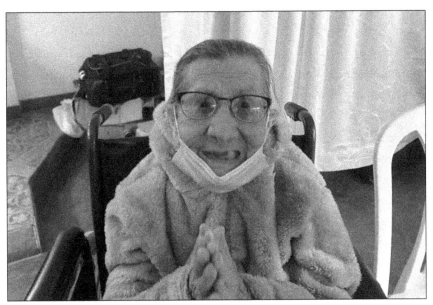

Paulina, a 94-year-old woman celebrating being able to see clearly for the first time in decades.

I came out for the second time and instead of returning to the clinic I just sat down next to Gabriel who was still lying down at the top of the stairs. I knew how she felt. My stomach was rumbling like an active volcano. I knew it would only be a few minutes until I would need to reenter the outhouse again. As I sat next to her while she was laying down on the top step of the outhouse, I noticed that there was a line of millions of ants marching across the ground, climbing up each of the steps, then over Gaby's stomach and down her back before proceeding into the outhouse.

I shook Gaby's shoulder.

"Gaby, you have a million ants climbing over your stomach and down your back."

In the years to come, I would experience all too often the bare truth behind her reply.

"I don't care!" she mumbled.

That day I realized that you're not a full-fledged missionary until you get sick enough to say, "I don't care!"

ONCE IN HAITI, WE WERE FORTUNATE ENOUGH TO be staying at a nice missionary complex just outside of Port-au-Prince. The compound was surrounded by eight-foot-tall walls, and it contained a large, manicured courtyard with green grass. I called this the Beverly Hills of Haiti.

While I stayed there I did something I normally don't do. I woke up very early one morning and walked out to the gazebo in the middle of this grassy courtyard to read my Bible. I noticed one of the women from our team was walking repeatedly back and forth in the far corner of the courtyard. Wow, I thought, she must have gotten up extra early and was spending the dawn taking a prayer walk. When she recognized me, she approached me. As she got closer, I could tell that she was crying.

"What's wrong?" I asked her.

"There's a bug in my room!" she said in a loud, frightened voice.

"Where is it?" I asked.

"It's in my sink and it's a COCKROACH!" she shouted through her tears.

"Don't worry, cockroaches can't hurt you. They don't even have teeth."

There was a Haitian volunteer in the gazebo with us.

"Oh, yes *dey do, dey* bite you!" he shouted.

Great, that's just what she needed to hear. She believed him and not me.

"What do you do at home when you see a bug," I asked.

"I leave the house and call my husband to come home. I stay gone until he gets rid of it."

Sometimes, I guess, Father tries to teach us how to deal with our fear by getting us out of our comfort zones … and some folks just may be better suited for less rugged types of mission work.

IN ECUADOR, WE STAYED AT A MOTEL HIGH UP IN the Andes Mountains. It had a unique architectural modification. There was a window in our shower that opened not outside but to the inside staircase. Everyone had to use that staircase to get from the first floor to the second floor. They all were able to walk by and say, "Hello." There were no blinds, no shades, just a peek-a-boo window looking right into our shower. I found an old painting on one of the walls in the motel. I took it down and placed it over our shower window so that we had a bit more privacy.

A year or two later we returned to that little village and our team stayed in that same motel. This time my wife Jennifer was able to accompany me. We had an "upgraded" room. The window in our bathroom did not look into the main staircase. Instead, it looked out to the street.

The only thing wrong was that the bathroom window had no glass, just an opening to the outside. At such a high altitude the temperature would drop down to thirty degrees at night. So, our entire room was thirty degrees in the evening. There was no way to heat your room due to no central heat and no fireplace. We just had a heavy, itchy, alpaca blanket, as thick as a rug, under which we tried to stay warm.

One evening after clinics, my wife was chatting in the lobby with the other ladies on the team and I decided to take a shower. There was no hot water whatsoever. I was bathing in an ice blizzard. I jumped in the shower, got a little wet, jumped out, soaped up, and then jumped back in, trying not to die from shock as the ice-cold water hit my body in a thirty-degree room.

I hurriedly dried off. I wanted to get my frozen feet off that wet, cold, tiled floor, but I couldn't get out of the bathroom. The door handle had broken. It would just spin and spin, but it never unlocked the door. Like in the movies, I tried ramming the door several times with my shoulder and it didn't budge. They make it look so easy in those movies.

Nothing I tried worked. There I was, wet, butt-naked, cold, and standing in a thirty-degree room on an iceberg of a floor. I couldn't get out. I started shouting in the direction of the window opening, which was at the top of the ceiling in the bathroom. I yelled in vain as no one heard me.

After forty minutes of wrestling with the door handle, I finally got it to work, and I escaped to the bedroom. I was shivering uncontrollably, and my feet were blue. Heat! Heat! I needed heat but there was none anywhere.

Then I saw it! Jennifer had brought a hairdryer with her, so I plugged it in, sat on my bed, still naked, and began to thaw my feet with it.

As I did this, Jennifer walked in and saw me naked blow drying my feet. "What the heck are you doing?"

I explained the entire story to her, and we still laugh about it today.

Later on that trip, I found a piece of cardboard I thought would cover up the window opening. I hoped it would help keep the cold air out of the room.

To reach the window, I had to stand with one foot on the toilet and the other on the sink as I stretched to reach the opening. Bad idea! The entire sink snapped off the wall, sending me and the sink to the ground. The porcelain sink shattered into a hundred little pieces on the floor. Then not only did I have a cold bathroom, but I also temporarily had one without a sink and a big mess to clean up!

IN HONDURAS, WE VISITED A CHILDREN'S HOSPITAL. We handed out small toys to the kids and prayed with their parents. It made me physically ill when I saw the conditions those kids had to endure. One of the nurses told me they didn't even have enough painkillers to give to the children as they recovered from surgeries or broken bones.

Three of us had to use the bathroom facilities when we were there. There was only one bathroom on that floor, and it was for both men and women to use. The lady who walked to the bathroom with us told us to go ahead of her. The other guy I was with used the bathroom first. He came out.

"Man, it's rough in there."

Then it was my turn. The entire floor was about an inch deep in urine. I had no choice but to walk in on my tiptoes trying to preserve as much of my shoes as I could. When I opened the doors to the stalls, I saw both toilets were filled to the brim with all kinds of nasty things floating in them. I had to pee so badly that I chose one of the toilets. As I peed, the fluids and other objects spilled over the top of the bowl onto the floor. When I walked out, both my friends who escorted me to the bathroom were waiting there.

"It's pretty bad inside there. Be careful," I warned my female friend.

She reluctantly decided to enter anyway. As soon as the door closed, my friend and I began to count.

"One, two, three, four, five …,"

She reappeared from the bathroom.

"I think I can wait," she said.

IN ECUADOR, ONCE WE WERE ABLE TO STAY IN A resort that was right on the beach. It was not the kind of resort you picture in your head when you hear that word. Let's just say their use of the word *resort* doesn't quite match our definition. Nope, not even close.

The first morning a couple of the ladies on our trip woke up to find they had been bitten hundreds of times each. Bedbugs! The place also had so many mosquitoes that when I stepped out of the shower, instead of grabbing a towel first, I would grab my bottle of repellent spray and drench myself with it. I had never had so many mosquito bites in my life. So much for resort life!

There have also been times when we had mice in our rooms. When a mouse runs across your bare feet as you walk to the bathroom in the middle of the night it will scare the bejesus out of you.

I even unknowingly brought one back home as a stowaway in my suitcase once. I wondered how many years I would have spent in jail for smuggling illegal rodents into the country if U.S. Customs would have discovered him. He survived the trip home by nestling in my clothes and eating some leftover snacks that I had in my suitcase. When I arrived home, I was emptying my dirty clothes into our laundry room and the little guy jumped out. It caught me off guard and I shrieked. I chased him with a broom and finally got him out into our garage. Jenn asked me what all the commotion was about, and I told her about the little mouse in our house. She began to yell.

"Get him out of here!"

"It's OK," I told her in my best Spanish accent, "Don't worry, our little friend, the Nicaraguan mouse, is now in the garage."

"Well, I hope an American cat gets him!" she replied.

Chapter Twenty-Five

THE HUG

At the location we went to in Honduras, many kids walked to school holding machetes in their arms. I thought about how that would never be allowed in our public schools, but here in this area of Honduras, it was the norm. As soon as school was over, they would walk straight to the fields where their parents were working and help them cut down the sugar cane. They would work late into the evening.

When we arrived at the school where all the machete-carrying kids attended, Jenn and I set up things in a single schoolroom. The room had no lights and only one opening—a few missing cinder blocks—for light to enter the room. The school chalkboard was old and missing most of the writing surface. Some of its corners were broken off.

Late in the morning, a woman came in. She had on a short-sleeved top and there were many large and bloody puss-filled white sores up and down her arms. I did not want to catch whatever it was she had. I didn't want to wait on her at all, but I did anyway.

I tested her eyes from a distance and made her new prescription glasses. I placed them on her head with my arms fully extended, staying as far away from her as I could.

She was grateful to be able to see and she leaned forward and extended her arms out to hug me. I remember leaning back away from her as far as I could, pushing my chair upon only its back two legs.

"Not in a million years would I let her touch me!" I thought.

But once again I heard Father speaking.

"Today, I don't want you just to do eyes. Today I want you to be my arms and hands. Hug her."

It was a clear message. I changed my attitude immediately and leaned forward to receive her hug. We embraced and she placed her head against my upper chest. She gave me not just a simple hug, it was a super-hug. She squeezed my ribcage tightly. I squeezed back and I realized at that moment that she probably hadn't held anyone for many years.

The hug only lasted for about two minutes although it seemed much longer, and it was magical. Compassion and gratefulness flowed through her into me, and I felt love radiating out of me. We were both consumed in love. Joy, peace, and love all combined into one big hug. It was as if God Himself joined us in a group hug.

Her eyes filled with tears. When she let go of me, she smiled, and without a word, she exited the building. After she left, I could still feel where her arms had wrapped around me for quite some time. Even as I write this story, I swear I can feel them again.

I was wearing a white scrub top that day. Afterward, I noticed it was stained with her blood and puss. I prayed that I would remain healthy. But even if I didn't, it wouldn't have mattered to me. That day I had just had one of the greatest moments in my life. When we hugged one another, we felt the presence of God. We had both been embraced by arms filled with love.

Chapter Twenty-Six
VOODOO CHILD

People frequently ask me "Of all the places you've been, where is your favorite to go to and hold eye clinics?" I usually reply, "I don't know."

I don't have a favorite country to go to. Each one is so unique, and everywhere we go the people are truly kind and loving. For many years I did have a least favorite place to visit and that was Haiti.

I've been to Haiti nearly a dozen times and my favorite time in Haiti was always when the wheels of the jet lifted off the tarmac as I headed back home. Every time I left, I found myself hoping that Father would never send me back, but on my last trip there, for some reason, I stopped disliking it so much.

There is, however, one thing in Haiti that I will never stop disliking and that is Voodoo. Voodoo is very dark and creepy.

During a God's Eyes clinic in the southern part of the country, I tested a young girl who was around twenty years old. She needed eyeglasses and while they were being made, I had a chance to talk with her. She spoke to me in English. I always love that because it means I don't have to use a translator.

We talked for some time.

"There is someone named Jesus who loves you so much that He died so that your sins may be forgiven," I shared with her.

"I know about Him. I know his name is Jesus. I desire to follow his teachings and pray to him and learn more about him, but I cannot do that."

"Why?" I questioned her.

"My father is a voodoo priest. He is the head priest overall in this area. Every time I tell him that I want to follow Jesus, he prays to the demons, and they come out at night, and they hurt me. I can no longer endure their torment, so I stopped wanting Jesus."

How was I supposed to respond to that? I never took Demonology 101 in college. I had no idea of what she meant by "the demons hurt me" but I was familiar with the verse in Ephesians 6:12 which probably best describes voodoo and other dark practices:

"For we wrestle not against flesh and blood, but against principalities, against powers, against the rulers of the darkness of this world, against spiritual wickedness in high places."

WE CONTINUED TO TALK FOR FORTY-FIVE MORE minutes. I can't remember much of what I said. I was just praying that Father would give me words that might comfort and encourage her. Afterward, I told her that we could ask Jesus to help her right now.

"Yes," she said, "I want that! I know I need to follow him, and I don't care what happens to me anymore. I just want Jesus so much! But … I can't go home because I will be severely punished."

We prayed right there, and she committed her life to Christ.

"Where can you go?" I asked her.

"I have an aunt who lives many miles away. She is a believer in Christ, and I know that she will help me, but I have no way of getting there."

I spoke with the pastor who was onsite with us and he promised to drive her there after the eye clinic was over.

Isaiah 61:1 says *"The Spirit of the Lord God is on me. The Lord has chosen me to tell the good news to the poor and to comfort those who are sad. He sent me to tell the captives and prisoners that they have been set free."*

THEY SHALL SEE GOD

The daughter of a voodoo priest was set free that day and Father used me to be a part of that. I love it when He finds me worthy of use.

Chapter Twenty-Seven
HARD TO BELIEVE

Several hours later in the middle of the night, after my time spent with the daughter of a voodoo priest, something happened that was extremely bizarre and evil. I will not elaborate on it here as it falls into a category that I call "things that go bump in the night." I've learned that these types of stories are best shared only with other missionaries. These stories involve the supernatural and are just too hard for many to believe.

Once in a different country in another remote village, many children warned me that anyone who sat on a particular rock would be visited by demons. I was tired after a long day of eye testing, and I wanted to sit down. I dismissed their warnings as foolishness and sat on the rock. Again, I won't go into any details here, but I can honestly say that they were right, and I had one of the most bizarre and frightening experiences in my life that night. There are unseen forces of good in our world, but I now know with certainty there are those of evil as well.

Stories that involve supernatural happenings are hard to believe especially when they involve evil, but they can also be hard to believe even when they are about good things.

In Acts 26, Paul writes of a supernatural event in which a bright light came down from Heaven that was brighter than the sun and it shone upon him and all who were with him. In that light, Paul says the voice of Jesus began to talk to him and tell him of things to come. When Paul recounted this story while on trial, he was interrupted by the Roman governor Festus who declared, "Paul, you are insane, your great learning has caused you to go mad."

Why is it that supernatural testimonies are often and so easily met with doubt or even flat-out disbelief? Some people I've shared stories with didn't even believe a single word I said.

When I once shared some of my stories of both good and evil supernatural events in detail with my dad, he told me, "I believe you only because you are my son, otherwise I would not believe you."

Once I shared a story of something I witnessed while I was in Africa, to a senior Bible study group of a large church where I had been invited to speak. The love they earlier showered me with quickly faded when I shared a story that turned out to be difficult for them to believe. They looked at me in the same way that Festus probably looked at Paul - like I too, was insane.

I have even had a church withdraw all their support from God's Eyes! They even canceled all their mission trips with us after I shared a story with them not nearly as difficult to believe as the ones that Paul shared above.

During the writing of this book, I've received great input from my friends and, although some close friends have encouraged me to write all of my stories, many have cautioned me to be careful what I include. I have decided that some of the hardest-to-believe stories would best be left untold here.

In the resurrection story found in the gospels, Mary met Jesus after visiting his empty tomb and He told her to go tell His brothers that He was alive. So that's exactly what Mary did. She went to the disciples and told them that she had just seen and talked with Jesus. His disciples, however, knew He was dead and now Mary brought them a difficult-to-believe story. Some did not believe her. What did Jesus do? He showed up later in the upper room and rebuked them for their unbelief (Mark 16).

We need to know that Satan uses doubt—it is one of his favorite tools. If he can keep us from believing that supernatural things take place, then he can prevent us from believing many things written in the Bible. Will Jesus rebuke us for doubting testimonies of supernatural events like He did to His disciples? Things that seem weird or hard to believe may be wondrous works of God. The Bible is full of such stories.

Chapter Twenty-Eight
DOWN THE DRAIN

One of the things that I enjoy most about what I do is that I get to meet some of the best people in the entire world. On one of my many trips to Honduras, we drove to the top of a mountain, and there I met a missionary couple and their children. They told me that they had operated a very profitable business back in the United States and they, like me, were from Georgia. They recounted to me that a few years earlier they followed a calling on their lives to leave their successful business behind and relocate to Honduras and serve the poor. I love discovering obedient people like them, whose actions back up their faith.

They were living in a small two-bedroom home in a little village in the middle of nowhere. They had learned how to dispense love. They were generous people and poured out kindness to all they met.

In their village, many children lived in very modest dwellings. Some of the children had only one parent, but several of them were surviving on their own without any parents. These missionaries had built this small house for their family, but on any given night several of the kids in that village would be sleeping somewhere inside that home.

Their home is where we held our eye clinic. It was as hot inside the house as it was outside. They had a small living room. Jenn and I refracted the eyes of the villagers in that small room.

One of the children who lived there was named Fernando. He was ten years old and wanted no part of getting his eyes tested or receiving glasses. Someone from the village, however, knew he couldn't see well, and they brought him to us to be examined. The testing revealed he was nearsighted and nothing he saw appeared the way it actually was.

We made him a new pair of eyeglasses and immediately he could see clearly for the first time in his life. As soon as I finished placing the glasses on him, he ran down the hall to the bathroom, threw his new glasses into the toilet, and tried to flush them down.

The missionary witnessed this and ran into the bathroom and grabbed the glasses out of the toilet. He then explained to Fernando why he needed to wear the glasses. He cleaned the new eyeglasses off and placed them back on Fernando's face. Begrudgingly, Fernando left wearing his new glasses and went outside. I'm guessing he probably threw them away somewhere else.

LATER THAT NIGHT AFTER AN UNCOMFORTABLE two-hour drive back to our basecamp, I was lying on a lumpy rollaway bed inside of a hot, stuffy dormitory room.

"If that's how people are going to react, I should have just stayed home in my nice, air-conditioned house and enjoyed my nice pillowtop mattress," I thought.

Fernando's actions continued to bother me. I kept trying to figure out a reason why he didn't appreciate the gift of good vision. Perhaps he was embarrassed by how they made him look, or afraid he would be teased for wearing them. Maybe he was just used to seeing things out of focus and he was fine with that.

I felt unappreciated for all my efforts, and I lay awake, allowing his rejection to rob me of sleep.

I DISCUSSED IT WITH JESUS IN MY PRAYERS. I TOLD Him how frustrating it was to see the way that Fernando and some of the others reacted to the gift I offered them. I told Him that I felt unappreciated for my sacrifice and saddened by how some of the children and even some of the adults would sometimes reciprocate my kindness and generosity with ungratefulness.

Jesus acknowledged to me that He knew exactly how I felt. He too continually offers a very special gift. The gift of love and forgiveness. The cost of His gift was much greater than my small sacrifice. He also had to travel to a faraway place and endure hardships to offer this gift.

Just like Fernando, some people don't want anything to do with His gift either. They are afraid of what they might look like as a Christian or perhaps feel embarrassed in front of friends, family, or business partners if they wore this gift of salvation openly in public. Maybe, like Fernando, they were used to seeing and living life without the gift offered to them and perhaps some of them conclude that the gift that Jesus offers is also waste that should be flushed down the toilet.

I shared Father's ache of rejection that night. He encouraged me with these words from John 15:18

"If the world hates you, bear in mind that it hated me first."

THE LESSON I LEARNED IS THAT JESUS KNOWS EXactly what we are going through. Our gifts may not be appreciated, but that should never deter one from giving.

⌣⌣

Chapter Twenty-Nine
BROTHER, CAN YOU SPARE A FORK?

We once held an eye clinic in a small desert village in Peru. It was one of the most unusual geographical places I've ever been to. This entire region is a desert made not out of sand, but rock and dirt.

Poverty there was abundant. The temporary residents lived in small shacks made out of literally anything they could find. Good thing it didn't rain there, or these people would get soaked.

We set up an eye clinic in a very small church about ten feet wide by thirty feet long. Believe it or not, somehow they had electricity so we had lights. The village was a squatter's village. None of the people living there owned the land on which they had built their shacks. They lived in one spot until someone told them to move. Then they would take their sparse belongings and set up somewhere down the road.

The pastor there walked through this squatter's village and asked everyone if they had a piece of silverware, he could borrow so that our team of nineteen would have utensils for our meals. The people were happy to help us, but in the entire community of hundreds of people he came up with only sixteen pieces of silverware.

Every night we had to turn people away from the eye clinic. There were long lines of people who waited for many hours. We dispensed about 900 pairs of new eyeglasses. We prayed for many eyes and people on that trip. We always told them that God loved them so much that he sent us to give them the glasses they needed. Many cried when their eyes were opened. Every day we received so many hugs.

There is nothing to do in this village. The area is so barren. Just look on Google Earth and you will see what I mean. Everything there is always covered in dirt, including the people. They have little and have little hope of ever making it out of there.

I realized on this trip that God's Eyes is an evangelical tool the church can use to grow. Every time we held a free eye clinic hundreds and even thousands of people showed up. Most people came in hopes of seeing better, but many of the villagers came just because it gave them something to do. God always uses the clinics to expand His kingdom.

This area was no exception. Someone told me that 124 of the townspeople prayed and invited Christ into their lives. The pastor of the church vowed to follow up with each of them. I jokingly thought to myself, he is probably going to have to start a church expansion campaign because there is no way all those new believers could fit in his existing church building!

It was there that I learned another reason that God's Eyes existed. We are here to help churches grow.

Chapter Thirty

A HEARTFELT MATTER

We finished a highly successful clinic in south-central Ecuador where we had helped over a thousand people. In one of the villages, the people were very small. The average height for adults was around four feet tall.

After the clinic was over, some of the people we had helped dressed up in their traditional ancestral costumes for us. They played music, danced, and served us snacks. Some of us quietly sang "follow the yellow brick road" to each other as it reminded us of the munchkin scene in the movie *The Wizard of Oz*.

This type of sendoff is always so uncomfortable for me because I know the poor are spending too much of their resources on us. We don't deserve to be honored like that. We come to serve the poor and yet it is they who desire to show their appreciation for what we have done. It's just too costly for them and I wish they wouldn't do it, but they are grateful, and it would be rude for us to try to stop them. I've learned just to accept their love, as they show their appreciation, and to embrace whatever way they choose to express their gratitude.

Many times, people have donated chickens to us. On the drive back to our base camp we once had six chickens on the bus with us. We gave them away to other poor families in different villages. I am always amazed at the extreme generosity of the poor.

On our way back home, we first flew to the airport in Quito and had a five- or six-hour layover. One of the missionaries hosting us suggested we go to the top of a nearby volcano to kill some time. We drove there and discovered there was a tram you could catch to the top of the volcano. To get there we had to park our car at an elevation of 10,000 feet, then walk up to an elevation of 11,500-feet to catch the tram.

I was sixty years old at the time, thirty pounds overweight, and in poor cardio shape. Five of us began the climb and I quickly fell behind the others. I was huffing and puffing. I told them to go ahead, and I would meet them at the entrance to the tram. Soon they were a few hundred yards ahead of me as we walked up the endless switchbacks. Eventually, they were out of sight.

As the oxygen thinned, my breathing became more and more difficult. I was sweating profusely, but I continued to push forward. I started to get light-headed and reached the point where I realized that something more was happening to me than just being out of shape. I saw little black dots revolving in circles around my head like the dancing stars in the old Daffy Duck cartoons when he was hit over the head. I knew I was about to pass out. I got down on my hands and knees so I wouldn't have far to fall. After a few minutes on my knees, I laid down on the road gasping for breath. My heart was beating like a jackhammer and for a moment, I believed I was going to die right then and there.

Eventually, I made it to the tram, but I was never able to catch my breath all the way and I couldn't slow down my heartbeat. I joined my friends and rode up to the top of the mountain. It was not a very wise move because the air at 15,000 feet was even thinner.

I enjoyed the beautiful vistas for a minute and then I found an empty bench where I lay down. My friends left me there and they hiked around for about an hour. I rested and sipped on some water and continued praying that my heart would slow back down. Gradually I was able to breathe more regularly and began to feel better.

I FLEW HOME THAT EVENING. A SHORT TIME LATER I went to see a cardiologist. I told him what had happened to me on the mountain, and he began to run tests on me. When he saw the results, he told me I had had a heart attack and I should be glad I was still alive. That information made me realize a few things. I had not been taking care of myself physically. After dropping our gym membership a decade earlier I had quit exercising and I was relying on Pop tarts, candy bars, and other junk food to get me through trips when the food was inedible or just not to my taste I had gained too much weight.

I also wasn't relying on prayer as much as I once did to see what trips Father wanted me to go on. I figured that since God's Eyes had the money I just started doing as many trips as I could. One time I did five trips in nine weeks. Every once in a while I would come home one day and leave a day later on another trip. I was always worrying if we had enough lenses made. I was burning out mentally, physically, and spiritually.

Some things had to change. I started eating healthier and began to exercise. I also began to pray more asking Father once again which trips to go on. It's so easy to be lazy both physically and spiritually I got ahead of God and just start doing things for Him instead of doing the things He wanted me to do with Him.

Chapter Thirty-One
MOZAMBIQUE

Several years after starting God's Eyes, we worked in South Africa for a few days offering clinics just twelve miles from Pretoria in an area known as Mamelodi. It is a place most people would not want to be in after dark. Hundreds of thousands of the world's poorest people live there in shacks and horrendous poverty.

For me, it was exciting to work in the slums there, but after a couple of days, it was time for us to move on. For the next leg of our trip, we planned to fly into Mozambique the following day.

While in South Africa, we were urged by the missionary we were staying with not to go to Mozambique because he said it was no longer safe to travel there. He had just given orders to all missionaries who were serving under his leadership in Mozambique, to evacuate the country immediately. He told us the country was on the brink of a civil war. Nine foreigners had been killed there that week and the violence appeared to be escalating quickly every day.

I remember thinking that I didn't travel all that way to Africa to not go to Mozambique. I felt the Lord had told us to go there and that's why we were on the trip. I told my missionary friend that, but he suggested otherwise.

"You better not go unless the director of the mission base you're staying at says it will be ok to come into that part of the country."

I tried calling the head doctor of the base whose number we had, but he didn't answer so I left him a message. We decided we would postpone the trip until we heard back from him.

He returned my call the next day after the plane we planned on flying on had already departed

"Is it safe enough for us to come?" I asked.

"How are you getting here?"

"We're flying from Johannesburg, stopping to switch planes in Maputo, and then flying into Pemba."

"As long as you're flying, I think you will be ok. But if you're driving, don't come. I don't believe you would make it here alive."

We only had to postpone our trip for one day. As it turned out this was a good thing because a plane from the budget airline we were flying on crashed later that day, killing all on board.

When I had booked the tickets, I selected the cheapest airline despite my wife's warnings not to use the no-name airlines in Africa. I had learned we could save around $90 by flying on this unheard-of airline with a one-star rating. I thought that it best suited our missionary budget. Since then, I've learned to listen to my wife.

We left the next day and I remember my friend Denny speaking to me:

"I'm glad we didn't fly the day before on that plane."

But I shattered his joy: "Yup, Denny that was good but we're now going to be flying on the same airline's *B* plane. The one that crashed was their good plane."

We made it to Pemba without any incidents. Once there, we discovered that the Pemba airport had only one set of airplane stairs for deboarding. We had to wait on the tarmac for around twenty minutes while the passengers disembarked on the plane that landed before us. Only then could the stairs be moved over to our plane.

As we waited, I took one of my favorite pictures ever. The runway worker who pushed the stairs over to our plane was wearing a work boot on one foot and a lady's pink flip-flop sandal on the other. Wouldn't OSHA have gotten a kick out of that! I think it also said a lot about just how poor this country was. This guy had a job, and he still didn't own a matching pair of shoes.

The Pemba airport terminal, at that time, was a large white military-type tent, and that's where we had to all stand around until we cleared Customs. I was grateful that they had a large fan that tried to cool us. After what seemed like an eternity, we cleared Customs and waited for our ride.

We were headed to Iris-Global Ministries. This mission group is headed by an amazing couple, Roland and Heidi Baker. They had been serving the poor in Mozambique for over twenty years. I suggest you look up Irisglobal. org and learn about their ministry. The stories of what Iris-global accomplishes are nothing short of spectacular. I had first met Heidi at a church I visited in Tennessee, two or three years earlier. I can honestly say she helped me grow much closer to Father and catapulted my walk with both Him and my journey into missions, to a completely new level. Roland and Heidi have started thousands of new churches in Mozambique, where Iris ministries feed over 30,000 people every day! I can honestly say I love and admire the level of intimacy they have with Father.

When we finally arrived at Iris Ministries, the temperature was over 100 degrees and the base housing had no air conditioning. The only food they served us was rice and beans, but they were the best-tasting rice and beans I had ever had. That was until I had eaten rice and beans for every meal for several days in a row. Finally, on the last day, they changed our cuisine. Instead of serving "rice and beans" we got to enjoy "beans and rice."

The mission base there is large. It's a 25-acre compound filled with an orphanage that housed a few thousand kids, schools, a library, a large pole barn for a church, which seats hundreds of people, and a small medical center. There is also a school for people who desire to go into the mission field. Every year hundreds of people, from all over the world, attend the mission school. These future missionaries attend classes from Monday through Thursday and are taught by some of the wisest, most well-known, and gifted Christian teachers, pastors, and missionaries in the world. They spent the weekends in the bush country. They would travel deep into secluded regions of Mozambique that have been seen by very few people. This hands-on training in tribal villages is invaluable to anyone who is considering missions as a career.

At the time of our travels, Mozambique was ranked as the second poorest country in the world. For a long time, before I arrived there, they had been experiencing a drought. It hadn't rained in over six months. There was no water coming out of any of the faucets or showers. Instead, they had to buy 55-gallon drums of water. We couldn't drink this water as it would make us ill. I remember paying $25 for a 12-pack of bottled water to drink.

Inside the men's bathroom was one of these 55-gallon drums. There was a cup floating on top of the water. We used it to measure out the two cups of water we were allowed to use each day to "bathe." It was ironic that we were in beautiful modern facilities with nice toilets and showers, but with no running water, so they couldn't be used. After pouring two cups of water over myself, I didn't even bother to dry off. One minute outside in the sun and I was dry, and after five more minutes, I would be drenched again in sweat. At times the temperature reached 113 degrees.

The outhouses we had to use were simple outhouse-type enclosures with concrete floors. In the middle of those floors was a four-inch square hole for you to squat over. My friend Denny joked that we should have taken Pilates classes before coming on that trip.

Mozambique had one thing in abundance, however, and that was flies. There were flies everywhere. I spent the first few days swatting them off. They would fly away only to land back on our bodies a few seconds later. After a few days, you stopped swatting because it was useless.

One night I spent time praying with three of my friends who had traveled with me... We spent around four hours in prayer and worship under a spectacular African sky. It was one of those times I refer to as "getting lost in God." That is how I describe it when one feels the presence of Father's Spirit so closely that you are unaware of how much time has passed. It is hard to describe that evening perfectly, but it created a deep peace and overwhelming joy inside of me that I had rarely ever experienced before. For lack of any better terms, it was magical. I wish everyone could encounter evenings like that

A little after midnight the four of us were sitting in a large, forty-foot diameter circular hut with open sides under a thatched roof. A girl in her late twenties walked up to us. We chatted for a while, and she told us she was attending the missionary school there.

"Who are you guys?" she was wondering. "I haven't seen you before."

"We've been invited here by Heidi. We feel like God is leading us to visit the medical clinic at the compound and hopefully add eye care to their services," I said.

"I have a story for you," she said. "I went to bed and fell asleep a few hours ago and tonight I had a dream. In it, I was shown the face of a man and was told that I would find him in the prayer hut. I was supposed to get up and go to the prayer hut to deliver a message from God to that man."

Then she pointed to me.

"You are the man I saw in my dream. God told me to share this word with you."

I was kind of stunned and I impatiently and joyfully asked what it was that she was supposed to tell me.

"Groundwork!" she said, and that was the only word she spoke.

Now "groundwork" may not seem like an important message from God. But for me, it was exactly what I needed to hear. Suddenly, my part in this whole crazy journey I had embarked on several years earlier, came into focus. I started God's Eyes and I have traveled all around the world doing eye clinics. Along the way, I discovered amazing people who wanted to become part of the God's Eyes team. I had also started bases in other countries where eye clinics could take place.

I realized at that moment that I had been doing "groundwork" for one of Father's ministries. This was my part in all of this - to do the groundwork that needed to be done for a ministry to grow. It seemed like Father was confirming everything I had done. To me, this message was a great encouragement to continue onward with everything I had been doing.

That night, under a beautiful sky, in the middle of nowhere in Africa, God amazingly spoke to me, through a stranger who I will most likely never see again. I knew without a doubt, though, that I was going to spend the rest of my life doing something so simple, yet at times difficult, dangerous, and incredibly humbling. I knew, however. it would also be wonderful, fulfilling, and important. I was to do … groundwork.

Chapter Twenty Two
LETTER TO DAD

Something important happened to me on a trip to Africa. God told me to write a letter to my father and tell him how much I loved him.

When I was young, we didn't use the word "love" very often at our house. It was a word that just was not frequently articulated. I don't recall my dad often saying that to my mom or my sisters or myself, so I thought that the letter I was to write would be a short one.

I did, however, recall one time when my father did tell me he loved me. When I was ten years old, I sold Christmas cards door to door in July to earn money. I bought a fishing rod at a garage sale for my dad with the money I made. I gave it to him one night when he came home from work late.

"Why did you buy me this?"

"Because I love you, Dad," I told him.

"I love you, too," he quietly mumbled back as he walked away down the hall.

Back then I was confident that everyone in our family loved each other, but we are of German descent, and we rarely expressed emotions openly to one another.

Something wonderful happened when I wrote that letter. I spent three days writing and rewriting it. The letter ended up being ten pages long. I was able to tell my dad how grateful I was for everything he did for me in my life. It was quite healing for me because, after writing it, I could then express openly

Jeff Catron and me freezing 15,000 feet above the equator in Ecuador.

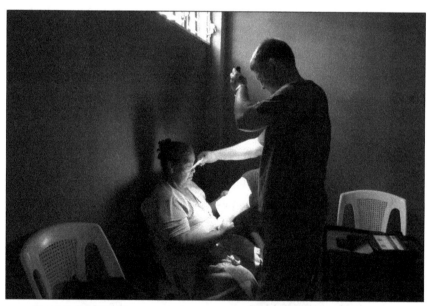

Dr. Michael Williams examining a patient by flashlight in Nicaragua.

how I felt towards him. Something inside of me changed when I wrote that letter. It made me feel closer to him than ever before. I kept thinking I didn't want him to die before he read the letter as he was already eighty years old.

When I got back to the States, I mailed him that letter. I thought he might perhaps reciprocate with a letter himself or at least a phone call. I was sure it would have a wonderful impact on him and that he would want to respond. I waited a month and heard nothing back, then two months, and finally three.

After three months I called him, thinking perhaps he had never received the letter. I thought it must have gotten lost in the mail. I considered resending it because surely, he would have responded by now if he had received it.

"Hi, Dad. Hey, I was wondering, did you ever get a letter from me that I wrote while I was in Africa?"

"Yes, I did."

I waited for more, but he didn't say anything. It was an awkward moment of silence.

"Well, what did you think about it?" There was another difficult pause. Finally, he replied.

"It was quite a letter … quite a letter." And that was all he said. But I knew that was a lot for him and it was enough for me.

I know he did not often share what he thought about anything. To this day I still don't know what his favorite food or color is. I don't know much of anything that he keeps inside of that brain of his. He is just not much of a deep talker.

But we now end every call with an "I love you." And that is all I need. I felt that something special came from writing that letter and it was worth taking the time to do so.

When I wrote the letter, I shared this with my friend Denny, who was in Africa with me. He said he wished he would have written a letter to his dad, but it was too late. His dad had already passed on.

"Denny, I feel that God is telling me that you should write the letter anyway. I think it will still do you some good." And he did.

Ephesians 4:32 encourages us to *"be kind and loving to each other and forgiving."*

And 1 Thessalonians 5:11 says we are to *"encourage one another and build one another up."*

PERHAPS WE SHOULD ALL WRITE A LETTER TO THAT special someone who needs to hear from us. Even if they've passed away, or even if it is hard to think of good things to say. It's good to pour out the love that lies within us. I can't help but think that someone who reads this needs to write a letter of love to a family member. Don't pass away with all those beautiful unshared words of love and gratitude hidden away and left unsaid inside of you!

Chapter Thirty-Three
A GREAT EXAMPLE OF LOVE

I've been to the Philippines many times. There, I met an amazing couple there named Joe and Billie. I have had the immense pleasure to work with them several times. We've held a few God's Eyes clinics in their house. They shun away from social media so few people have ever heard about them. Today they are both in their seventies or maybe in their eighties by now, battling failing health.

What makes them so special is that decades ago they moved to a small island in the Philippines and adopted a child they found abandoned on the streets. Then they adopted another and another and another. For the past several decades they have continued to do this and at the last count, I know of, they had adopted 163 children!

They do not run an orphanage. They just have a home and an exceptionally large family. They adopted those abandoned and abused children and gave them all the same last name. Now each one of them has a mother and a father who loves them. These kids never had to leave home at a certain age. They could stay there forever because they are part of the family. Some are now adults and in their forties and some have chosen to stay home and help with the younger kids.

Almost all of them had been sexually and physically abused before they were abandoned and left to fend for themselves. Many had physical disabilities, as some are blind, and several cannot walk. Others had even greater impairments, but this couple, Joe and Billie, loves them all. Their love tanks are full. They pour out love in the way Father intends for us to do. They are living sacrifices. I am in awe of such people.

In the book of John, Chapter 15, Father commands us:

"Love each other as I have loved you. There is no greater love than this, to lay down one's life for his friends."

JOE AND BILLIE HAVE DONE THIS. THEY HAVE SPENT their lives pouring out love so that others may live. Every time I'm with them I just want to spend hours talking with them. To me, their lives are not only exemplary but a constant source of encouragement. They are gifts to not just their 163 children but to us all.

∪∪

Chapter Thirty-Four
CHICKENS IN CHURCH

One Sunday morning in Uganda our group divided up into three teams and each team visited a different church. The group I was in attended an Anglican church. It was held in a large pole barn type structure with a huge, thatched roof that hung down until it was only a few feet from the ground. This open-air structure had no doors, and you could enter the church anywhere by simply crawling under the roof.

Once inside we were escorted up to the stage, which was a massive rock about four feet tall and thirty feet long. On this natural stage, we sat in small plastic chairs like those you might find in an American elementary school.

The pastor welcomed us and, although he knew how to speak English, the service was held in their native language of Tesu. When it came time for the offering, the people walked up to the stage with their gifts. A few brought cash and laid it on the rock, but most of the people were poor and they brought whatever they could. Some brought a dozen eggs while others could only give one or two eggs. A few people even donated chickens. Still, others donated handfuls of whatever crops they were growing. By the end of the offering, there was a giant cornucopia of vegetables on the stage.

It was such a humbling and beautiful moment watching these impoverished people bring their gifts to the Lord. Well over a hundred people attended the church that day. After everyone had given something, the pastor would pick up an offering item and auction it off to the highest bidder. One man bought a chicken, carried it up to where we were seated, and laid it in the lap of Julia, one of the girls in our group. We all laughed hysterically, except Julia, who was the recipient of this new feathered friend.

At one point in the service, the pastor turned to us and said, "Now we will pray." The entire church got down on their knees as the pastor prayed, so we did as well. We were not kneeling on soft dirt but knelt painfully on that huge rock. I thought our knees would have felt better if they had been resting on pointed daggers. After five minutes, my back was also screaming for relief. I tried every position to ease the discomfort, but it was to no avail.

There's an old church joke that goes, "I could have listened to you pray all day, and for a moment I thought you were going to." The pastor must have had an overabundance of prayer requests he addressed because he prayed and prayed and prayed. After what felt like thirty minutes, he turned, nodded slightly, and spoke just to us in English and in his very deep African voice he said,

"This concludes our first prayer."

Then he turned back to his congregation and began to pray even more.

I whispered loudly to the other team members.

"Did he just say the FIRST prayer?"

They couldn't hold back their laughter. For the next few minutes, someone was always snickering. The pastor prayed a second and eventually a third prayer.

By that time, I was certain that knee and lower lumbar replacements would be in my near future.

The service was so looooong that I wanted to introduce them to the American one-hour church service limit. Halfway through the endless sermon, Julia looked at me with a puzzled look on her face and whispered:

"What am I supposed to do with this chicken on my lap?"

Her expression was priceless. I bit my lip to keep from bursting out in laughter.

"You don't have to hold the chicken. Its legs are tied together so it's OK to put it on the floor. It can't run away."

For the rest of the service that poor chicken laid on the hard rock in as much discomfort as we were in when we were praying. I'm certain it, too, was praying that the pastor would stop talking and that this long-winded servant of God wasn't even considering a closing prayer.

Chapter Thirty-Five
GET OUT OF HERE! *NO MAS!*

Serving on a God's Eyes trip is a great thing to do. When my heart and head are in the right place, serving is a joyful experience. Those days are wonderful as love and kindness pour out effortlessly from me. I treasure those days. Towards the end of a long trip, however, exhaustion eventually settles in and joy seems to elude me and hides far from my reach.

On one trip to the Philippines, we held clinics in a different village almost every day. Some nights, after seeing patients for eight to ten hours, we would drive again for hours until we arrived at the next sleeping destination. As soon as we got there, we attempted to grab a few hours of sleep before waking up shortly after sunrise only to start another long drive to wherever it was that we were holding the next clinic. Then we would set everything up before seeing patients again at eight in the morning.

On the final day, late in the afternoon, I thought we had finished seeing all of the patients and I packed up my supplies. I was dog-tired but pleased that we had finally finished seeing everyone. That satisfaction was short-lived, however, as the director of the school where we were working came in with several more students who had finished classes late.

"There's only a few of them. Will you please see them?"

We unpacked our supplies and equipment, helped them all, and again put away our stuff.

Then a family, who had walked all day, arrived and asked us to help them. They were followed by several others. Once again, we unpacked everything to help everyone out. After we finished packing up for the third time, I was finished mentally, and I was spent physically. I was so tired and hot.

I just didn't want to do any more testing as I had reached the end of my rope. I began to think of the long forty-hour trip ahead of me to get back home to America. I made up my mind that no matter who else came in that day we were done. I had hit my wall. There was nothing left in me to give, and I was becoming very grumpy. I told my translator to close the door to the room we were working in, stand in front of it and make sure that no one, and I meant no one, under any circumstances, would be allowed to enter.

As I began to pack up everything for the fourth time a young girl, perhaps twenty years old, came up to me.

"I haven't been helped yet," she said softly.

I angrily shouted to my translator who was supposedly barricading the door: "Who let her in?"

I glared at the girl. Her apparent innocence didn't have me fooled.

"How did you get in here?"

"I have been here for a very long time, but no one ever called my name," she quietly answered.

I nodded for her to sit down in the empty examining chair. I wanted her to notice my frustration about having to help her, so I loudly unpacked the examining equipment once again.

I begrudgingly tested her eyes and discovered that she was the most nearsighted person I had seen on the entire trip. Out of the hundreds we saw, this young girl desperately needed glasses more than anyone else. I finished refracting her and sent her over to get her first pair of eyeglasses.

As I waited for her to return from the crew that assembled and dispensed her glasses, I thought of how I had wanted to tell her to leave. She had done nothing wrong. All she had done was to wait patiently until someone helped her. I began to agonize when thinking about how many years she would have had to live with poor vision if I had sent her away. It could have been years, or maybe she never would have had her vision corrected in her entire life all because I was tired. How many times does Father have to teach me this lesson?

Galatians 6:9 teaches us, *"Do not grow weary of doing good."*

Ashamedly, I had done exactly the opposite. Father humbled me and I let Him know once again how sorry I was for the way I acted. Somehow a small amount of energy came back and all I wanted to do was be kind to her and let her know she was loved and important. I told her how sorry I was for the way I allowed my weariness to get the better of me.

She was extremely happy to be seeing clearly and so was I. Once again, I learned how much better I needed to become. Father has shown me that when I'm tired, He will strengthen me and continue to use me to be a blessing if I would only ever learn to follow His teachings.

Chapter Thirty-Six
OBEDIENCE 101

I have a friend from church who owns and operates a real estate firm. One day she approached me at church and shared a story.

"I've got a contract on a house I'm selling, but am having trouble with the closing."

She needed it to make her month's goal, but no matter how hard she tried, it looked like it was going to fall through.

"One night I was praying about the situation," she excitedly told me and continued. "The answer surprised me. God told me to go with you on a trip to Haiti. I couldn't believe that I heard God's voice!"

She was beaming with joy.

"I heard His voice! I heard His voice! I'm not going to go, BUT I HEARD HIS VOICE! God talked to me!"

I was delighted by her joy but also a bit puzzled. Her enthusiasm was awesome, and she was so excited about hearing Father's voice, but she didn't care so much about the message. There was no way she was going to go to Haiti because it scared her too much. Suddenly, I realized how much she and I were alike. I love hearing Father's voice as well but oftentimes I don't want to hear the message He speaks. There are times when I am not in any hurry to do what Father asks me to do.

A few weeks later she changed her mind and decided she would be obedient and go on the trip. It was a frightening step for her. She always had a huge fear of being kidnapped and raped. Haiti would not be the first choice for a destination to travel to if you have those kinds of fears.

On the second night of the trip, we traveled to a small, secluded village in the southeast corner of Haiti. It was late at night and dark outside by the time we finished dinner and continued on the trip. One of my dear friends Rick, and I joke back and forth when we are on mission trips together by saying "What could possibly go wrong?" Well on this trip we were about to find out. Our van's engine began smoking heavily and we stopped moving. Some of the guys got out and discovered the engine had overheated. When our Haitian driver took off the radiator cap, steaming fluid exploded all over him and splattered antifreeze all over the engine. One of our team members badly burned his hand. There we were dead in the water in the dark of night in remote Haiti.

At this point, my realtor friend had a panic attack. She believed this was the moment that she had always feared was about to come true. One of the pastors on the trip tried to console her, but it didn't help very much.

I had hoped to ease her fears by saying, "Don't worry. Three hours from now we'll be safe in our beds at the compound."

Yeah, those words didn't comfort her at all! Her apprehension and panic remained. But thank the Lord panic attacks don't last forever.

About thirty minutes after the breakdown, a local man driving a motorcycle came by and saw we were broken down. He stopped and offered to help us. Strangely enough, he had exactly the tools needed for the necessary repairs. He duct-taped up the tear in the radiator hose. He did not, however, have any radiator fluid and all of ours had spilled out.

He left and returned with a five-gallon plastic bucket filled with water balanced precariously on his motorcycle. He filled up our radiator.

As we continued our trip we knew we could only drive so far with a radiator filled with just water and no antifreeze. We still had over an hour of driving to do. I thought the engine temperature would head into the red zone on the temperature gauge and that the taped-up hose would probably not last long. We all silently prayed during that last hour as we kept our eyes on the temperature gauge. Somehow, we made it! As we rolled into the compound the engine died again.

We unloaded everything and headed to our bunkhouses. I looked at my watch and it had been exactly three hours since our SUV first broke down. It was just as I had predicted earlier to my friend. I told her she would be safe at the compound in three hours. If only she had believed me, she could have had some peace.

During that trip, the Lord began to work on several of the other fears she had. I could see her faith growing. I was proud of her for not only celebrating her experience of hearing Father's voice but also for her obedience to walk out something she was afraid to do. I knew that Father would reward her for this act of obedience, and He did!

Her faith continued to grow and just a few years later, she and her husband would later walk away from their successful careers. Today they have dedicated their lives to full-time Christian service working with Fellowship for Christian Athletes.... just not in Haiti!

Chapter Thirty-Seven
FRANK

Frank was an optician working in Haiti at a place where God's Eyes was supplying eyeglasses. I think he was in his late forties when I first met him. A few days after our initial meeting I returned home to the States.

He occasionally kept in touch with me and one day he told me his story. For over twenty years he had tried to get a visa to come to America but could never get one. He said the visa application fees cost $130 and it would take him almost two years to save up that much money. He had applied thirteen times over the past twenty-some years and every time his visa application was denied. He was disappointed with his government for wasting his hard-earned money, but he always had a dream to visit here. He asked me if I would write a letter to the Haitian Embassy asking them to grant him a visa, which I did.

A few months later he notified me that his visa was approved and that he was coming to the States. Someone in Indiana had bought a ticket for him so he could go visit them for several days. I was glad for him and wished him a good trip.

Many weeks later I received a call from Frank. He was in Florida at the airport, and he wanted to come to Georgia and see me. I wasn't expecting him, but I said, "OK," and then he said, "Great! Now you must buy me a ticket to get there."

THEY SHALL SEE GOD

I wasn't planning on that either. I didn't even know he was on his trip to the States and I didn't remember him mentioning anything about his desire to see me when he came to America. I did, however, agree to get him the roundtrip ticket from Miami as he requested. He flew up to see me that evening. He planned to spend three days with us before returning to Miami and then onward to Haiti. I picked Frank up at the airport around 10 p.m. and we headed to my home.

"What did you have to eat on the plane?" I asked him.

"Nothing, food costs money on *de plane*," he said, looking a little ashamed.

"How much money have you brought on this trip?"

"None," he answered.

"Ok," I thought. "I guess I wasn't only going to pay for his airline ticket, but everything else for him as well.

We passed a McDonald's on the way home. It was the only place open that late at night, so we pulled in.

"What do you want to eat?"

"What do *dey* have here?"

It struck me at that moment that he had never heard of McDonald's before. At that time there was not a single McDonald's franchise in all of Haiti. I believe that's true to this day. He decided to get a chicken sandwich meal and I ordered a hamburger meal for myself. The total came to a little over nine dollars and Frank felt bad.

"We should not have eaten here," he said.

For Frank, nine dollars was a lot of money, certainly much more than two meals should ever cost.

At home, we put Frank up in our guest room. The following morning, he came downstairs.

"May I take shower?"

"Of course," I told him, "Just use the shower in the extra bathroom upstairs next to your room." Frank used the shower for over forty-five minutes, and I began to wonder what was taking so long.

When he finally came back downstairs, I suddenly realized what took so long. Forty-five minutes is how long the hot water lasted before it turned cold. He had just enjoyed a hot shower for once. He probably only had a few hot showers in his entire life.

I asked him what he would like to eat for breakfast, and I'll never forget how he responded.

"It is not for a guest to demand what to eat."

Wow! in the States, we don't think twice about requesting what we want to eat.

"I can make you eggs and bacon, or oatmeal, or cereal or"

He interrupted me enthusiastically.

"You have cereal here!"

"Yes, of course, we do." I think that most people who have children in the States probably have several boxes of cereal in their pantries to choose from."

I took him over to our walk-in pantry.

"Help yourself to whatever you want. We have several choices of cereal."

As he entered the pantry he said, "You have rooms just for food?"

With each of his questions and answers, I was humbled as I began to see things through Frank's eyes and not my privileged ones, which took so many blessings for granted.

Frank pulled out boxes of Fruit Loops, Frosted Flakes, and Raisin Bran. I showed him where the bowls were. He didn't grab a cereal bowl; he grabbed a large salad mixing bowl and he emptied all three boxes into it at the same time. I was amused by how delighted he was, ecstatically devouring his crazy breakfast.

For the next few days, I took Frank around town. In one of our conversations, the subject of auto insurance came up.

"What is insurance?" he asked me.

"Well, auto insurance is when you pay money to a company that will cover the cost of repairs for your car in case you ever get in an accident."

"What happens if you never get in an accident, you get your money back, right?"

"No, they keep it," I chuckled.

He thought that was unfair.

"There is no way that could ever be legal!" he declared.

His answer made me think that Frank should run for office. I would certainly vote for him!

One night I took him to a local gathering that we call "movie and a message." About twenty guys from several different churches get together, eat pizza and wings and then we watch a movie and discuss it afterward.

The gathering was held at a friend's home in their nicely furnished basement which had plenty of room to watch movies. It was complete with a large screen TV, surround sound speakers, and many comfortable chairs and couches on which you could relax and watch the movie. This was almost too much for Frank to comprehend.

I told him to help himself to all the food he wanted, which completely blew his mind. I mentioned all this was relatively common where I live and that many people I know have movie theaters in their basements.

"What is a basement?" he asked.

The movie we watched that night was "Facing the Giants." Frank was as excited as a kid running through Disney World for the first time. He jumped up and down out of his chair cheering on the football team as they were running to score a touchdown. His emotional outbursts were, however, a tad bit annoying to some of the guys. Some seemed quietly disturbed about it.

During a sad part in the movie, Frank wept out loud like a baby, so much so that his wails were drowning out the soundtrack. I had never realized the magic and power of movies before. After watching hundreds of movies while growing up, I suppose I had become desensitized to those emotions. That night it made perfect sense to me why the "*Jesus* film" had such an impact on people who hadn't seen a movie before.

We took up a collection that night and blessed Frank with it. The next day he asked if I could take him to buy a portable battery-operated DVD player so he could play movies at his home. Frank's modest house in Haiti had no electricity.

While driving around, Frank told me that after having two children he decided to get a vasectomy because he knew he couldn't afford any more children. I've been told that in certain parts of Haiti your status as a man is elevated by the number of children you produce, not by how many survive or by how many you can take care of. He said he was sometimes ridiculed by his country's people who called him "Frankcastraty." All this was because he chose to be a responsible man.

Frank's brother had many children. I forget whether Frank said it was eleven or thirteen, but I know he cannot afford them. In the evenings while Frank and his family are eating, his brother's children come to his small home and stare in the windows because they are hungry. Frank told me he rarely finishes a meal. Usually, he only eats half of it and then gives the remainder of it to his brother's children so they would have something to eat that night.

My wife, Jenn, was a high school teacher at the time Frank visited us, and she wanted him to speak to her classes. After he spoke, the students were allowed to ask questions.

"What kind of precautions do you take when a hurricane hits?" one of her students asked.

"We don't know when a hurricane is coming ... it just comes."

Frank left us after three days. I told my wife I was glad.

"I don't know how much more I could have taken of his sad stories of the hardships he has to endure." Frank helped me realize how much I take things for granted.

When I first met Frank, he had upset me with the way my prescription lenses were not being used. However, after spending a few days with him, I was sympathetic towards him due to all the difficulties he encountered in his life. I had judged him without knowing his world. He is only one of many people in this world who try to do the best they can with what little they have. The real fact was that Frank was a good man who just had limitations due to his poverty. Over the next several years I came to realize the poor should not be pitied but rather should be admired. They are so much stronger than we are.

Matthew 7 teaches us: *"Do not judge, or you too will be judged. For, in the same way, we judge others, we will be judged, and with the measure we use, it will be measured to you.*

Chapter Thirty-Eight
TAKE MY HEART OUT AND SMASH IT

One time in Panama I talked with a man while I tested his vision. I asked him how he was doing. He told me he was hungry. I asked him why and he told me that he had not eaten in three days. I once again asked him why. He told me his vision had gotten so bad he could no longer identify food in the garbage dumpsters he searches in. Wait a minute? Did he just tell me his vision has gotten so bad that he can't identify food anymore in garbage dumpsters! OMG!

Tears immediately filled my eyes. How much more can my heart take? How is this even possible? I gave him the glasses he needed to solve the seeing part and some money to buy some food, but all too soon the money will run out and he'll be back in those dumpsters looking for food to survive.

ANOTHER TIME IN NICARAGUA WE HELD AN EYE clinic in a large church. By midmorning, we were sweating from the heat. The church had air conditioners, but the pastor couldn't afford to turn them on for us. He said it costs thirty dollars a day to run the air conditioning. I paid him immediately and within an hour the church started to cool down.

A BIT LATER THAT DAY I MET A MAN WHO HAD DIA-betes. He said he no longer took medicine for it because he couldn't afford it.

During his eye exam, I told him he needed to find a way to get back on his medicine because if not he would soon have even worse trouble than just having poor vision from the disease. That's when he told me the following words:

He said, "I know, I can no longer feel my feet when the rats eat them at night."

AN HOUR OR SO EARLIER I GAVE A PASTOR THIRTY dollars so I wouldn't have to tolerate high temperatures inside a church. And now I had a guy sitting in front of me whose poverty was so extreme that his feet were eaten by rats at night. Those words still haunt me today. Imagine waking up with bloody feet because rats have dined on them during the night. What kind of shack must he live in? What kind of suffering must he endure? I was ashamed of what I chose to spend my money on. How could I put my comforts above helping to alleviate someone's suffering?

IT WAS ONE OF THOSE MOMENTS WHEN I KNEW I had to do something more than give him eyeglasses. I had a few hundred dollars in my wallet. I always take as much cash as I can on trips for moments like this. When I brought his new glasses over to him, I gave him everything I had and told him it was a gift from Jesus. I spent the next hour praying with him and his wife and telling them that the next world could be much better. He and his wife cried and hugged me the whole time. You would have thought I gave them millions of dollars. When in fact all I did was offer them words that gave them hope for their future. This is why I take all these crazy trips. We must help those who cannot help themselves.

Chapter Thirty-Nine
GOBSMACKED

Another time in Mozambique, missionary Heidi Baker, took us to a nearby Muslim village. As with many villages in that country, this place was the living definition of poverty. I have seen lots of poverty throughout my travels with God's Eyes over the years, but this place was right up there with the worst I had seen.

As we walked through that compound, many children recognized Heidi and ran out to greet her. She always returned their joy and excitement with hugs of love which she has learned so effortlessly to give. The children followed her wherever she walked. I have never seen so many children that happy just to be around someone before. As we walked through the village Heidi would purchase whatever anyone happened to be selling. She usually handed whatever she bought to the group of children who engulfed her. One time she bought a small bag of peanuts.

Somewhere along our stroll, we came across a tiny little lady, maybe in her seventies, who recognized Heidi and she also joined our strolling entourage. After she walked with us for a few minutes this little lady invited us to her home, and we all accepted. We walked over to a small shack made from dried mud and manure with a straw roof. Her home was extremely small, perhaps only five feet wide by six feet long, and the entire structure was probably only four feet tall.

The four of us from God's Eyes, Heidi, and the homeowner squeezed inside of it. Three of my friends and Heidi sat on the smallest and most uncomfortable-looking bed I have ever seen, while I sat on a small table the size of a footstool. This was all the furniture she owned.

The little lady squatted down and leaned gingerly against one of the dried mud walls. Heidi gave the lady the bag of peanuts she had just purchased. This extraordinary kind little lady counted out the peanuts and gave each of us five of them, keeping none for herself. We were shocked by her generosity. One of the guys with us handed his peanuts back to her so she would have something to eat, but that's not what the lady thought. She bowed her head in embarrassment and shame, thinking she had forgotten to peel the nuts for us. So, she shelled the nuts and handed them back. I was speechless and dumbfounded. This frail little lady had just given away ALL her food to us.

All five of us sat there gobsmacked. I couldn't even talk. She was easily one of the most impoverished people I had ever met, and yet she just gave us everything she had.

We talked briefly as Heidi translated and we asked Heidi what happened to these shacks during the monsoon season? She told us that after a few days of hard rain these shacks simply dissolved and then this tiny lady would have to spend the rest of the season outside with no shelter at all in the rain. This was all too much to hear. One of my friends told Heidi to tell the lady that he would buy her a house so she would be kept dry even during the monsoons. He kept his word and paid for the small house that Heidi's mission built for her.

Without any expectations of reciprocity, this lady gave us all she had, and Father repaid her with a much finer home. It would be built with masonry blocks and have a waterproof aluminum roof that would withstand the monsoon season.

To this day I still can't believe what I witnessed. I think in all my travels that was the moment I was touched the most and I will never forget the generous heart of that impoverished little lady.

Chapter Forty
LADY AT PUBLIX

Back in the States, I was at a Publix grocery store buying a can of soda. It was the only thing I was buying, so I was looking for the shortest checkout line. I settled in a line with only two people ahead of me. The lady ahead of me bought several items, but she was almost done. The second woman in line had only a few items, so I thought it wouldn't take too long.

As I stood there waiting for the first lady to leave, I heard the checkout woman tell her how much everything would be.

"Wait, I have food stamps," she said, and began rifling through her purse for something.

I live in a slightly affluent area, and people there tend to be somewhat well dressed most of the time. This lady, however, did not look like most of the other people. Her hair wasn't perfect, and she had on an old loose-fitting, spaghetti-strapped T-shirt. She was just not as polished as some of the other people in the store. It didn't bother me, but it appeared to have disturbed the lady standing behind her. Through her stares, she seemed to be judging her as being "beneath her" solely based on her appearance.

Whatever she was looking for in her purse took quite a while to find. I began to look at the other lines to see if they were moving any faster. Then I heard the Lord speaking.

"Does it matter how quickly you get back to the office? Will an extra few minutes be worth changing lines for?"

"Not really", I replied to Father, "I'm not in any particular hurry."

"Just wait here," He said, so I did.

The patience of the lady directly in front of me, however, had worn thin. Her waiting time limit had expired. She became agitated. She loudly reloaded her items back into her cart.

"How dare she shop here and waste all our time!" she said rudely and just loud enough for the lady in front of her to hear. She angrily excused her way past me and headed for another checkout lane.

Finally, the lady in front of me found what she had been looking for. The cashier entered something on the cash register and gave her a new total of twenty dollars and eighty-four cents. She then began searching for change in her purse.

"Give her twenty dollars," the Lord said to me.

I tapped her on her shoulder and handed her twenty dollars. I told her that the Lord wanted her to have this money.

She looked puzzled.

"Why are you giving me this money?

"God wants you to have this."

"Did you hear that? God wants me to have this money!" she said to the cashier.

She thanked me many times before leaving.

I finally checked out and purchased my bottle of soda.

"It was so nice of you to help her," the lady cashier whispered to me.

"Believe me, it wasn't my idea. I'm not that generous or kind, but God is."

When I exited the store, the lady I had given the twenty dollars to was waiting for me. She was crying.

"I want you to know that I'm a single mom and I was just laid off from my job this week. When I came to the store today, I had no idea how I was going to buy both food for my family and gas for my car."

As she was telling me this, Father reminded me that someone earlier that week had blessed me with a 100-dollar bill, which was still in my wallet. He

The spot where Glenses worked so hard and invested all his time serving God.

*Lady rummaging for food in a garbage dump
next to a God's Eyes clinic in the Philippines.*

told me to give that to her as well. As she was crying and telling me her story, I pulled out the hundred.

"God wants you to have this too!"

She hugged me and thanked me over and over. I let her torrent of tears soak my shirt.

"Are you rich or something?" she asked through her tears.

"Nope, I'm just a missionary."

"Where do you go to church?" she asked me.

At that time, I was attending several different churches. I invited her to the closest one, but I said that where I went to church was not important.

"What is important is that you realize that God loves you so much and He wants to get to know you better."

After that, she gave me another round of hugs and a thousand more thank-you's and then we headed towards our cars. As far as I know, she never went to that church and that doesn't matter. What matters is that a lady enduring a very rough time in life was blessed by Father that day. He cares dearly for her and loves all of us very much.

I went back to work realizing I had just paid over $120 for a small bottle of soda, but that was just fine with me. We are asked to store up treasures for ourselves in Heaven and not here on earth!

Chapter Forty-One
GLENSES

One day while sitting at my office desk reading emails, an elderly gentleman walked in.

"Hello, my name is Glen."

"Welcome to God's Eyes," I said.

"I'm interested in doing some volunteer work for you. I'm 89 years old and have been having some trouble finding anyone who will allow me to volunteer."

Because of his age and health concerns, most people wanted him to stay at home.

"They just want me to sit in a corner until I die. I just have to have something to do. I don't want to spend the rest of my life sitting on my butt all day."

My first thought was that life and old age was getting the best of him and that maybe he should just take it easy. He was unsteady on his feet and attached to an oxygen tank with tubes going into his nose. We sat and talked for an hour or two. From the energy in his voice, I could tell that he hadn't given up on life. He was a delightful man with alert, sparkling eyes. His mind seemed very perceptive.

"I'd like to come in and help maybe one or two days a week for a couple of hours," he explained.

One job we have at God's Eyes is sorting reading glasses and bagging them up to be sent all over the world to doctors or missionaries who will distribute them. A large group from a local church came by every month and spent a day doing this for us. I figured that would be something he could handle and he could sit down at a table because it wouldn't be physically demanding for him.

Glen did that a couple of times for us and one day he walked over and studied our edging machines.

"What do these machines do?" he asked.

"We have to edge every lens blank that comes in so that they'll fit the frames we are using."

"Can you teach me how to do that?"

I thought it might be a bit much for him to learn as it would require him to stand at the machines in order to use them.

"That may not be a good fit for you."

"But I would like to learn it."

I finally decided we'd give it a try. I remembered reading an article that discussed how it's smart to spend fifteen hours training someone to do something that will save you fifteen minutes. I took a chance and spent hours teaching him how to do everything.

Glen learned quickly. Later he learned to use all the other machines in the lab as well. His body was growing old and weak, but his mind was not. One day a week became two days a week, then three, four, and five. The only time he didn't come in was when I was on trips. Every time I returned, he wanted to know all the stories about the people who received the glasses he had produced.

One day while I was packing up for another God's Eyes trip, Glen spoke up.

"How about giving me the key to this place so I can cut lenses while you're away."

I hesitated. I thought if he died cutting lenses while I was gone, I might come back to discover his corpse lying on the office floor. I didn't want to give him a key, but Glen had a soft way of convincing me to take a chance on him.

He jokingly made me a promise.

"If I feel like dying, I'll walk outside first."

He had a keen wit and sense of humor.

We spent many hours laughing as he reminisced about his life with me. He was always cutting lenses. Almost every day.

My son enjoyed bringing my little grandsons in occasionally to visit. They nicknamed him "Glenses" because Glen was always cutting lenses. He even learned to operate two machines at the same time, doubling his productivity. He had his way of doing things and I would have to tell all the other volunteers not to touch anything on the machines Glen used.

"Don't even think about moving anything that has Glen's name on it." It became a funny thing around God's Eyes, and I can't remember how many times I had to tell people, "That's the screwdriver that Glen uses!" or "That's Glen's Sharpie!" or "Don't touch Glen's stuff!"

Glen passed away at ninety-three. He refused to just fade away. His final years were exemplary of how one can and should finish life. He worked at God's Eyes almost every day until the day he died. At his funeral, I thanked his wife for sharing Glen with me for all those years.

"What you didn't know, Bryan, was that he loved it so much he would have paid you to let him be there," she told me.

Dang it, I joked silently to myself, *If I had known that I could have made a lot of money!*

I miss Glenses a lot.

Chapter Forty-Two
WHO'S GOT SENSE?

I'm including this story because it taught me another thing I needed to learn if I was going to be a successful leader of one of Father's ministries.

Three years into my leap, my son said he wanted to talk with me.

"Dad, I'm thinking of asking my girlfriend to marry me."

I reacted quickly.

"No way! You are not going to ask someone that you've only dated for three months to marry you. What you need to do is date her for at least a year or preferably two years. After doing that if you still want to get married, then that's when you ask someone … it would just be foolish to get married after such a short time of knowing someone."

He did not react immediately. After a pause, he responded.

"Dad, why are you speaking death into my love?"

It was profound. How would I ever reply to that? I knew he had just spoken wisdom.

Later that night I had a talk with God about the afternoon conversation with my son.

"I was just giving him fatherly advice. You know I love him and don't want him to make a mistake and get hurt."

He spoke to my heart.

"Instead of reacting immediately and giving him fatherly advice, you should have taken the time and responded to him with Father's advice." I didn't even ask Father what He thought about them getting married. I just reacted and started babbling. How can I ever know what God has planned if I don't even pause to ask Him.? What if He was planning for them to be together? What if He was going to use them to raise money for God's Eyes. I have NO idea of what Father has planned unless I ask Him. I didn't even consider Father's desires before I replied to my son.

"Well, I was speaking common sense to him," I told Father. "Common sense says not to rush into marriage."

Then God responded to me with one of the most profound answers I have ever heard, and I've quoted this a thousand times since.

"BRYAN, WHY WOULD YOU SPEAK 'COMMON SENSE' when you could have spoken 'God sense?' If what you speak is common sense and not God sense, then what you speak is NON.... sense."

OF ALL THE PEOPLE IN THE WORLD I KNEW NEEDED to get this lesson down pat, it was me. I am the one Father has selected to lead one of his ministries. Why would I ever want to only speak common sense? Father longs to share his wisdom with us and it is far superior to anything I would normally say or think.

So how do we get God sense? You read His words, learn them, and apply them. You bring your common sense to Him first before you reply. You learn to run everything through Father before you speak or act. It only takes a second and once common sense has been run past Father, He will approve it, or He will correct it, and then it becomes God sense. Over the past decade and a half, I've learned that common sense, not surrendered to Father, is often the antithesis of faith.

HERE'S A POSTSCRIPT TO THE ABOVE CONVERSATION. As of this writing, my son has been happily married for eleven years now to

Janelle, the girl he told me he wanted to propose to. They have three wonderful children, and I am incredibly blessed by them and proud of all of them!

Chapter Forty-Three

THE BEST PEOPLE

I first met my good friend, Geoff, at a gathering called NOF (Night of Fellowship). Every Saturday night about fifty people from many different churches would gather to love and encourage one another and share testimonies of what God was doing locally and throughout the world. Many missionaries who served all around the globe frequently attended. Geoff was one of several people who led worship there. He was one of those people who can do everything well. He was a gifted musician, had a beautiful voice, and was an IT guru and an airplane pilot. He owned an airplane and took me flying just for fun several times. He told me he loved the stories I shared about the God's Eyes trips I've taken and said he wanted to come on a trip with me sometime.

His first trip was to a small village in central Ecuador with a large team of doctors and nurses from Texas. Once there, we discovered that the governor of that region disliked Christians and she forbade us to help any people in the town. Basically, the trip was a bust. The medical team was unable to hand out even a single pill and God's Eyes didn't hand out one pair of eyeglasses.

Geoff wasn't discouraged. He joyfully led us in worship each night. Father somehow still used that broken trip to ignite a deep fire in Geoff for mission work. Over the next few years Geoff and his wife, Joy, began to travel with God's Eyes around the world.

They are probably the brightest and kindest couple I've ever met. They quickly learned everything I taught them while Father took them on a deeper walk in their spiritual lives. Eventually, they retired from their successful careers and moved to the country of Panama as full-time missionaries where they hold God's Eyes clinics.

They expanded the good works that God's Eyes had begun there years before. They formed a large team of both medical and non-medical volunteers. Their mission grew until they were holding eye clinics nearly every other week throughout western Panama. During the Covid-19 crisis, when the shelter-in-place laws stopped the eye clinics, they temporarily switched from eyeglasses to handing out meals to the poor, whose lives were severely impacted by strict government mandates. In only eight months they purchased, gathered, and helped pack and deliver over 300,000 meals to people who had little or nothing to eat.

Geoff and Joy are dear friends and one of those special humble couples in the world who have learned the secret of dispensing love and hope seemingly with little effort.

Chapter Forty-Four
GIRL IN A BLUE-STRIPED SWEATER

As I've written before, I believe everyone has a story. I love listening to people's stories, but some people are facing nearly impossible situations. Often, I hear unhappy accounts—accounts of hopelessness and despair—and I become filled with sadness and heartache. When this becomes too overwhelming for me, I usually find a quiet corner somewhere or walk outside and just cry. Sometimes I question Father as to why they must endure such difficulties. Other times I just pray for them through my tears. How many eternities must pass before all this suffering goes away?

People tell me all the time that what I do must be so rewarding. I usually reply, "Yes," but learning about people's misery also makes it the most heart-wrenching thing I've ever done.

In my office on the wall behind my desk, I have around 150 pictures from trips I've been on, arranged to spell the word, *Love.* I just looked at one of those photos and it reminded me of another one of those heartbreaking stories I encountered.

WE WERE SEVERAL HOURS SOUTH OF GUAYAQUIL, Ecuador, high up in the Andes Mountains. Usually, it's very hot where we go, but this time we were at an altitude of over 8,000 feet and it was extremely cold outside. A mother came into the clinic with her nine-year-old daughter. The sad-eyed little girl was wearing a heavy, blue-and-white-striped wool sweater that her mother had knit for her.

After the two of them had their eyes tested and they received their new glasses, the mom told me about her and her daughter's story.

The little girl had a brain tumor that was cancerous and growing rapidly. The day it was diagnosed was the last day the mom saw her husband. He abandoned both, blaming the mother's genetics as the cause of the daughter's illness. Since they had been abandoned and were without any means of income, they had been forced to move back home to her parent's house in the mountain village where we were. Just a few weeks after they moved back home, both of her parents died, and she and her daughter were once again all alone without any means of support.

The doctors had said her daughter didn't have much time left and the medicine that might prolong her little girl's life cost hundreds of dollars per month. He might as well just have told them it would have cost her millions. She had nowhere close to that kind of money. She was just going to have to let the tumor advance until it would take her daughter's life. Holding her in my arms, I prayed with her, then walked outside and began to cry.

I've heard far too many of these tear-jerking stories while serving in third-world countries where someone has had to endure incredible hardships. There are few tragedies worse than not being able to afford the medicine that would save your child's life or ease their suffering. To bear such hopelessness is unimaginable. Yes, what I do is rewarding, but at times like these, it is emotionally crushing.

"How many more tears do I have left?" I wondered.

"As many as you need," Father softly whispered.

I LEARNED LATER THAT IT'S OK TO CRY BECAUSE Father promises in Psalm 126:5 that *"They that sow in tears shall reap in joy."*

Chapter Forty-Five
THE CUSTOMS OF CUSTOMS

Traveling to developing countries around the world can be challenging, especially when dealing with some customs agents. I'm sure there are many decent and honest customs agents in the world, but when you enter some third-world nations, the chance of encountering corrupt officials increases exponentially. There are some agents I have encountered that look at you as their next meal ticket.

On one of my many trips to Haiti, I encountered one of those agents. Our group was taken to a back room for "processing." We had a large group carrying in a lot of medical, dental, and eye care supplies. I was about fifth in line for inspection. A few of those traveling with us had only clothes in their suitcases and they went first. They were quickly cleared and told to stand behind a yellow line about ten feet away from the rest of us.

Before that trip, I had been warned many times not to declare the actual value of the equipment and supplies I was bringing with me to Haiti. If I did, I would possibly be charged some exorbitant amount to get the equipment and supplies through.

I have had equipment stolen or confiscated by corrupt agents before, so this time I tried a new approach. When it was my turn to have my bags opened, the guard inspecting my bags turned away for a moment. I quickly kicked the bag, which had many thousands of dollars worth of eye testing equipment, over to one of my friends standing behind that yellow line. It was a perfect kick and my suitcase coasted smoothly across the room, over the yellow line, and stopped right in front of my friend who had already been cleared.

"Wow, what a great break," I thought. Now all the equipment was safely through.

The guard turned back around and opened one of my suitcases containing several hundred pairs of reading glasses. You would have thought by his reaction that it was filled with cocaine. He immediately got a flat cart and asked me which bags belonged to me. As he was loading them up my friend who was behind the yellow line watching over the "safe" suitcase filled with all the equipment, spoke out.

"Hey, this suitcase is his too!" And he even brought it over to the customs agent!

I shot him an angry glance like the one my mom used to give me when I was a kid and I did something wrong.

"Just wait till I get you home!" I thought.

I had successfully glided the most valuable suitcase safely across the yellow line without inspection and he just brought it back to me.

The guard told me to follow him, pulling my many suitcases with him. Then he put the suitcase he had previously opened on a counter.

"How many glasses are in here?"

Well, I know how this game is played. He was going to ask me for some ridiculous amount of money.

"In the suitcases, there are 400 pairs of reading glasses."

"How much *does* each *one cost?*" He spoke in his broken English.

I remembered what I was warned to do. If I was asked this question, I would declare a greatly deflated price of fifty cents per pair.

"Oh, *you gonna* have to pay lots of money for *dat.*" He had to get a calculator to do the math. "Four hundred times fifty cents is $200! You owe us money on that $200 worth of supplies."

I had maybe $40,000 total worth of eyeglasses and equipment in my remaining suitcases. I hoped that since I was cooperating with him and answering all his questions, maybe he wouldn't open any more of my suitcases and discover the rest of the equipment. Thankfully, he never opened the other suitcases, but he walked away and left me there for a few minutes, and then he came back.

"On $200 worth of glasses, the duties and tariffs will cost you $1200. You must pay me in cash."

This is how you can tell if the agents are corrupt. The corrupt ones always demand cash. He had "calculated" the whopping rate of 600 percent fees on what I declared.

I was very glad I didn't say $40,000, and this is exactly why I was told not to declare full value.

"We are here on a mission trip. I am giving everything away to your poor countrymen for free and I shouldn't have to pay those kinds of fees!"

"Too bad, my friend, those are *de rules.*"

I kept arguing with him. He stood his ground.

"*Dis* is the law. You have to obey it."

I knew it wasn't the law. Six hundred percent duty tax was way out of line. This wasn't my first rodeo with crooked agents. We fought over the fees for a couple of hours. Occasionally, he would do what most corrupt agents do…he would eventually lower the amount and tell me a new figure.

Finally, the leader of the medical group I was with came in and said we had to get going. It had been hours since I had been detained in Customs.

"There is no way I am going to pay the fees you want! I will break every single pair of glasses I have, and I will throw them in the garbage can before I pay you," I declared in a not-so-kind voice.

The leader of the trip interrupted and asked me how much he wanted. By this time his price had whittled down to $272.

"Let's just pay it, because we need to get going." She told him she would pay for it herself, which she did, and we eventually headed on our way.

Unfortunately, sometimes, there's no other way to get through.

I HAVE BEEN TO PERU OVER A DOZEN TIMES. SOME groups we work with have arrangements with Customs there and we get through

The girl in the blue striped sweater was one of the thousand people we helped in Saraguro.

Jeff and Joy Catron holding a God's Eyes clinic in a small village in Panama.

very easily. Sometimes any kind of official-looking papers with signatures and stamps on them written in English would get us through. Other times we explain that we are giving our supplies to the poor. They tell us they are poor too and they want some of what we have. I usually say, "Help yourself."

When I make an offer like that, several of the agents come over and grab handfuls of sunglasses or reading glasses and then they allow us through.

Peru has a red light/green light customs system. You press a button and randomly the light turns red or green. If it's green, you just take your bags and proceed through, but if it's red, all your stuff gets searched. I've been told by some Peruvians that the agents will just keep whatever they want for themselves, and then they will allow you through.

Once I was there with a church group and I was the last one through the customs area. Before I got to the red and green light machine, an agent inquired as to what was in one of my hard-sided suitcases. I told him I had eye testing equipment in it. He gathered all my suitcases, then told me to follow him.

We walked for twenty minutes to the back of some part of the airport. There I was taken to a counter and was asked how much everything I had was worth. I gave him some numbers, but he questioned everything I said. He took out all my equipment, looked up the model numbers, and priced everything on the internet.

He then walked me over to a small ten-foot by ten-foot room. There was nothing in the room except a table with fold-up legs and a few plastic chairs. He told me to sit down, and he read me what he had printed on some forms.

The bottom sheet of his stack of forms said I had to pay $4,050.

"You must pay me in cash."

"I don't have that much. I only have $100 on me."

That was the truth, I then questioned him and spoke.

"Who brings $4000 in cash with them when they come to Peru? One time when I was here, we were robbed. Ever since then I've only carried $100 cash with me whenever I come here."

He quit talking in English and he began yelling at me in Spanish. Then he walked out of the room intentionally slamming the door behind him so hard that the walls shook.

A few minutes later he came back.

"You must give me $3,800."

"I don't have that much." Once again, he started yelling at me in Spanish and slammed the door as he exited.

A few minutes later he repeated the same demands.

"$3,200 is final."

"I only have $100," I said with outward calmness, but inward with fear and some anger.

This went on for over two hours and each time the demand for cash went down a few hundred dollars. Each time I told him I didn't have that much. He just grew angrier and angrier. After hours went by the total demand for cash had been lowered to $156.

In total frustration, I took out my wallet and pulled out my five twenty-dollar bills. I held open my wallet in front of his face so he could see that it was empty. Next, I pulled my pockets inside out from my pants to show him I didn't have anything else on me.

I stood up and as I simultaneously slammed the five twenty-dollar bills, one at a time, on the table I said, "This! ... Is! ... All! ... I! ... Have! What don't you understand?"

He once again stormed out of the room.

I put my money back in my wallet and sat down. Another fifteen minutes went by and finally, the door opened. This time two armed police came in. They firmly gripped my arms beneath my armpits and lifted me to my feet.

"Come with us!"

As I was being escorted to somewhere else in the airport, I grew apprehensive.

"This is just great! I came to Peru to help the poor with their vision and now I'm being arrested and taken to jail," I thought to myself.

For another twenty minutes, I walked with them, one on each side of me firmly holding my arms at the elbows. What were they thinking? That I was going to make a run for it? Finally, they led me up to an ATM.

"Withdraw $156," they commanded. The machine only allowed withdrawals in twenty-dollar increments so I took out $160.

Then once again, in the same manner, I was escorted back to the sparse room where I had been. I sat back down at the table. The police left and a minute later the man who originally demanded the $4,050.00 from me came back in and told me to give him the $156.00

I handed him eight twenty-dollar bills. He counted the money.

"I will bring you your change," he said, and he left.

I thought to myself "What is going on here? Has he become an honest thief? He's now worried about giving me back the four dollars I just overpaid him?"

Five minutes went by and he returned as promised and handed me four one-dollar bills. I thought he probably took them from another person he was holding hostage in some other room.

"You're free to leave now!" he demanded.

I collected my suitcases and someone else escorted me back to the original Customs area.

I eventually found some people from my group who had waited inside the terminal for hours for me. They took me to the bus where the rest of the team had been waiting during my ordeal. My suitcases were loaded underneath the bus and we finally began our trip.

WE DROVE SEVERAL HOURS OVERNIGHT TO THE village where we would be working. We arrived early the following morning. Upon unpacking the bus, I realized that one of my suitcases was missing. Someone who loaded it, or someone along the way when we stopped for gas, took it. I'll never know, but it was gone forever.

It was the second time in Peru that I had to go without a change of clothes. I remained in the same outfit for almost the entire trip. This time, however, I decided to forego the purchase of tight-fitting Inca Devil attire.

"I suppose Jesus didn't change outfits often either," I thought.

My wife Jenn, however, was to bring another group down ten days later. She was to meet up with me in Lima. I called her and asked her to bring me another suitcase full of clothes. When she landed at the airport, she texted me.

"Hey, Baby, well, I got here fine, but Delta lost one piece of luggage somehow on my non-stop flight … guess which one?"

I just laughed, of course, it was the one with my extra clean clothes in it.

ONE TIME WHILE IN ZAMBIA, CUSTOMS AGENTS confiscated my autorefractor. This is a portable piece of equipment that helps us know what lens power a person needs to see clearly. At that time portable autorefractors cost $15,000. All the other supplies made it through, but even after pleading for hours with the customs officials, they would not let me have the most important piece of equipment I had brought with me. Without the autorefractor, we would still be able to help people, but it would take much longer, and we wouldn't have some of the measurements needed to provide an accurate assessment of their vision needs.

After another long argument, they said they would keep the autorefractor in the Customs warehouse while I was in the country and that they would return it to me when I left the country. So after the trip was over I arrived back at the airport and walked to the customs warehouse to retrieve my equipment. It was ten minutes away.

When I got there, I met with the Customs agent.

"You are not allowed to export this machine to the United States."

"But it is mine. Can you tell me why?" I questioned.

"Because it was never imported into Zambia. You cannot export anything that hasn't been imported. "

"But when I arrived here, they wouldn't let me import it. They took it from me," I explained,

Customs were sticking to their story that I couldn't have it.

"What do I need to do to get my auto refractor back?"

"First you must fill out papers to import it. Then get those papers approved. Then fill out papers to export it and get those papers approved. After you have done that, only then will you be allowed to have your machine back."

When I asked for the import/export papers, I was taken to another building and given the papers which were written in either Bembe or Tonga. (Those languages all look the same to me.)

"How can I complete these forms when I can't read them?"

Someone in the group I was with offered to translate for me, and he said he would be willing to stay and help me. I was so grateful for him. I remember he said I should leave the negotiations to him since he was Zambian, and he knew how to deal with the customs agents.

He received no argument from me. I thought that was a perfect idea and immediately agreed. Down the hall from where we were was the office of the head of Customs. My friend decided to go straight to the top and talk with her directly and get everything settled quickly. I followed him as he confidently marched straight into her office while she was talking on the phone, and we waited about five minutes until she hung up.

My friend started explaining to her how we were attempting to retrieve my autorefractor and the trouble we were having.

She snapped back at him in an angry tone.

"How dare you barge into my office without an appointment and interrupt me on a personal call!"

"Get out of my office and leave me alone!"

She escorted us to the door and slammed it behind us. (It seems door slamming is a universal talent of Customs agents.)

Oops, so much for that approach. I couldn't help but think that aggravating the head director was not going to be beneficial in obtaining my equipment. My translator friend then said we had no choice except to hire one of the "customs expeditors" who were available for such situations. After some haggling, one of the expeditors agreed to assist us for a price of 150,000 quatras, or about sixty U.S. dollars.

An hour later the expeditor came out.

"I cannot finish the paperwork."

"Why?" we asked him.

"I have already done 150,000 quatras worth of work. No more work until I'm paid more."

He had us over a barrel at this point and my translator friend renegotiated a new amount with him. I paid him more money and he disappeared into the back offices.

My plane was going to depart soon, and I knew I was going to miss my flight if I didn't get back to the airport.

"How much longer will this take?" my friend asked someone there.

Not much longer, we were told.

After thirty more minutes, we were still nowhere near done. I walked back to the airport to tell my friend Todd and the rest of his team to go back to South Africa without me.

"I'll be fine because I have a translator with me. I'll catch the last flight to South Africa in about four more hours." Todd reluctantly agreed and the team flew back without me.

THERE I WAS IN ZAMBIA BY MYSELF. I STOPPED AT the airport ATM and got some more money just in case I would need it. Upon my return to the Customs office, I found my translator friend arguing with our expeditor who was once again demanding more money. My Zambian friend was getting quite upset.

He looked at me with fire in his eyes.

"I have had it with these liars. They are breaking every agreement I make with them and I'm leaving." And that is exactly what he did.

He left me alone with the expeditor who pretended to only know a little English and spoke it only when he felt like it. I was left to fumble around trying to communicate with him.

"Give me ... more money!" he said. I understood that part!

I gave him some more and the scene continued to repeat itself over and over until I was out of money again.

Once again, I took the ten-minute walk back to the airport terminal and I took another $200 out of an ATM. I proceeded back to the Customs building again. I paid the expeditor more money and once again he disappeared into the back room.

It had now been over three hours since I first arrived. My expeditor came out. "Why don't you just leave the equipment here. It's not worth all the hassle."

We had told him earlier when we had to declare the value of the portable autorefractor that it was only worth around $800, not its actual value of $15,000.

"I know it's not worth much, but it has sentimental value to me. I'm not leaving without it," I insisted.

Every twenty minutes he came back out and said he needed more money - Some for the girl who must type the papers, some for the girl who must enter everything into the computer, some for the guy who stamped and sealed the papers. Some for the guy who printed the copies, etc.

Once again I made another trip to the airport ATM for more money and after about four hours, two men came out and told me all sixteen pages of paperwork were finished and approved and I could get my equipment released.

They walked me over to a large warehouse building that was filled with goods and paraphernalia to the ceiling. The place looked like a Walmart, Sears, and Home Depot combined. There were washers, dryers, couches, recliners, flat-screen TVs, bicycles, ATVs and so many suitcases you couldn't even count them. You name it and it was there.

I was lucky. I noticed my autorefractor case sitting about eighty feet into the warehouse in a row with hundreds of other black suitcases. Fortunately, it had a large emblem on it that I recognized. I went to get it, but I didn't know that only the expeditors could go into the warehouse. A guard who was there waved his semi-automatic rifle at me and shouted at me to stop. I immediately concluded it would behoove me not to argue with him. I couldn't believe it. Finally, after almost five hours and $440 worth of paperwork (bribes), I got my autorefractor back.

For icing on this miserable cake, the two expeditors who escorted me to the warehouse, then said I owed them an additional 50,000 quatras each for the retrieval of my case. I told them I had no money left and they said no problem. They would walk with me back to the airport ATM.

"How is America?" one of the guys asked while escorting me back to the terminal.

"America is wonderful and beautiful," I told him. "Everyone in America is very wealthy. We all want to come to Zambia and help out all the people here, but we can't because of PEOPLE LIKE YOU!" I snapped!

I had lost my patience and replaced it with a bad attitude. I blew it again. The Bible teaches in James 1:20 *"For a man's anger does not bring about the righteous life that God desires."*

I believe that! But sometimes it just seems impossible to do and so once again I blew it.

IN AFRICA, MANY THINGS ARE OFTEN DONE SO DIF-ferently and so inefficiently as compared to how things are operated in the U.S.A. Many times you end sentences by saying, "T.I.A." which stands for "This is Africa!" That's just the way it is, and Zambia was no different! Situations there can seem utterly absurd. There's no sense in complaining because complaining will not change a single thing about how things are done.

Delta charged an extra $150 to change my flight and about forty minutes later I was finally on the plane. On the flight back God had a chat with me about not getting angry at people and how to love people the right way. I had no idea of the hardships of living in a developing country like Zambia. I shouldn't criticize or judge someone because of their actions. If I had to walk in their shoes, who knows, I may have acted in the same way and forced others to pay me.

Todd was at the airport when I got back to South Africa. He was relieved that I had my autorefractor with me. He had sent out a chain prayer request to many people asking them to pray that I would get it back safely. I was glad that God honored those prayers.

In every country we go to, we have our in-country ground crews check with government officials to see what needs to be done for us to bring in supplies.

Sometimes when they call Customs, even the customs officials say they have no idea what we must do. Sometimes what you must do changes every few days and sometimes it just depends on the particular agent you get as to what they believe has to be done. If there are forms to fill out or get approved, we do that. I have no problem paying tariffs or duties if they are required by their laws. It's giving money to corrupt agents that make it so infuriating.

STILL, I HAD TO LEARN THAT EVEN COMPLETING ALL the required steps doesn't always get us through. Once in Nicaragua, the agents wanted to keep all the prescription lenses we brought with us. We showed the customs officials that we had permission from their government to bring in the supplies and showed them our approved paperwork. They told us that even though we had the paperwork they weren't sent the paperwork they needed on their end. They wouldn't accept the completed and the approved forms, with stamped seals from their government, that we had with us. They told us that since it was Friday night, nothing could be done until the government offices opened on Monday. They could, however, immediately expedite the situation for the low, low price of $400.

We said no to that, and we were forced to leave our prescription lenses with them. Someone on our team returned to the agents on Monday. That didn't work out and they tried again on Tuesday which didn't work out either. Finally, we had to hire a Nicaraguan attorney to solve the problem for us on Wednesday. He was able to help us for the low, low price of only, you guessed it, $400.

IN SOME COUNTRIES, EVEN WHEN THERE ARE NO required forms to fill out, we've had customs agents stand in front of us and demand that we need "papers" to get through. "Papers," I learned, is a euphemism for money.

Sometimes if it's late at night or we're on a tight schedule, I usually respond accordingly.

"Oh, I didn't know I had to fill out papers. How much do the papers cost?"

If they give me an amount of $100 or less, I usually just pay them, and they allow us to move right along. Sometimes if they say I have to go over to another area located to the right side of the room for more hassle, I just turn left instead and exit Customs. This has worked for me many times and I have saved a lot of money in "bribe payments" by doing that.

USUALLY, BEFORE A TRIP, I ASK SEVERAL PEOPLE I know to please pray for us at the approximate time we will be going through Customs.

We have had what I will call "favor" offered by many of the agents. When we tell them that we are there to help the poor in their country to see, they simply wave us on through. Some even thank us for coming.

In one country where we had previous trouble, many people were praying for us. When I put the suitcases, containing supplies, on the conveyor belt to be X-rayed, the agent for seemingly no reason at all just got up from his chair and walked ten feet away. He then stood with his back to me for as long as it took for all the supply suitcases to go through the X-ray machine. As soon as the last suitcase containing supplies passed through, he again, for no apparent reason, returned to his chair and X-rayed all the other suitcases for our group which only contained their extra clothes!

ONCE IN PANAMA, ALL OUR SUITCASES MADE IT through X-ray without any problem at all. I was so excited everything went through that I asked my wife to help me wheel all of them out of Customs before anyone changed their mind. We exited Customs quickly. Once the rest of our group cleared, we made a long walk to where our friends had parked their cars. We loaded up the cars and I noticed my backpack was not there. I realized I had left it on the conveyor belt in Customs because I was in such a rush to get the suitcases out of there.

If you've ever been through Customs, you'll know it's a one-way process. You can only leave Customs; you cannot re-enter through the doors you exited. By this time, we were on the opposite end of the airport, a twenty-minute walk from Customs. The chance of ever retrieving my backpack was not looking good, so I began to pray. One of my friends from Panama accompanied me to see if there was anything that could be done to retrieve my backpack. I prayed silently as we re-entered the airport on the domestic side of the terminal opposite the Customs area we had initially exited through.

Just after entering, I saw what looked like my backpack sitting alone on a table. I went over, grabbed it, and opened it. It was mine! Nothing had even been taken! My computer, my wireless headphones, and all my medications were in there!

How did it get there? Who carried it from Customs and placed it on a random table on the opposite end of the airport from where we had exited Customs? Who knew what door we would come back into the airport through? Why did there just happen to be an empty table there with only my backpack on it? And why was everything still in my backpack? To me, there was only one answer. It must have been that Father orchestrated the entire event. Things happen when we pray that wouldn't happen if we didn't..

Chapter Forty-Six
EATING AN ELEPHANT

Sometime after moving to our new headquarters, I received a call. The conversation went like this:

"Mr. Kaiser, you don't know me, but I want to donate some new lenses to your organization. Would that be okay?"

"You can do whatever God is telling you to do." That's the way I always answer when I'm asked those types of questions.

"I wanted to make sure you have enough room for the donation."

"If we don't, I'll make room. How many lenses are you sending me?"

"I believe it's around 200,000 lenses."

I couldn't believe what I was hearing. I knew that 200,000 lenses would take up somewhere between twenty to thirty pallets. Two hundred thousand lenses are worth a lot of money, probably millions of dollars at retail value.

"Why thank you so much!" I calmly answered while jumping up and down, clicking my heels, and giving high fives to invisible people!

"I'll be in touch shortly," he said and hung up.

He had called me on a Friday and that weekend I told a lot of people what had happened. We were getting 200,000 new uncut lenses donated to God's Eyes. He called me back the following Monday.

"Mr. Kaiser, I apologize, I have made a mistake."

In the back of my mind, I kind of knew that already. No one would donate 200,000 lenses. He must have meant 20,000 or maybe just 2000, which would still be a huge amount. I began to think that I would have to tell everyone I was wrong about the size of the donation.

"What is the correct amount?" I asked him.

"It's more like 500,000 lenses."

I was in shock. Where in the world would we house 500,000 new lenses? The retail value of those lenses was astronomical. There are probably only a few wholesale lens dealers in the entire country with that amount of inventory. In a single phone call, God's Eyes was going to receive one of the largest inventories of lenses in the nation.

When the lenses arrived, our warehouse director, Denny, and I would joke about how we would ever sort so many lenses. While sorting, we frequently joked, "How do you eat an elephant?"

"One bite at a time!" we would respond in unison.

How did we sort 500,000 new lenses? One pair at a time. It took us over a year to categorize all those lenses and sort them into hundreds of plastic bins.

I once again was reminded that there is nothing too hard for God to do. He can even fill an entire warehouse full of new lenses.

Ephesians 3:20 teaches us that "He can do immeasurably more than we can ask or imagine."

SHORTLY AFTER RECEIVING THE SHIPMENT, I ASKED Father.

"Why didn't you send the lenses a few years ago?"

"Bryan, you were not ready for them until now."

He had to test me to see how I was handling what He had been giving me. A donation of this magnitude only arrived after years of affirming that I would pour out what He poured in.

Chapter Forty-Seven

TEN PENNY NAIL

On one of my many trips to Nicaragua, I became ill and began to vomit. I thought it must have been something I had eaten. I threw up over and over, yet this time, things seemed different to me than the other times I had had food poisoning.

This time, besides the vomiting, I had a lot of extreme pain in my lower intestines. I was heaving so hard and loud that I woke up some of our team members staying five doors down from my room. I felt especially bad for the three other guys sharing a room with me. I knew I was keeping them up all night.

At one point after vomiting so frequently, I decided not to return to my bed but chose to lie down on the dirty bathroom floor. I was in such pain and vomiting so hard that after a while I couldn't sit up to throw up in the toilet. I lay on the floor and threw up all over myself.

The next morning one of my roommates came into the bathroom and saw the mess I had made.

"Bryan, you're lying in your own puke and it's all over you!"

"I don't care!" I mumbled.

I remembered Gaby in Ecuador, with ants all over her, saying the same thing. I also remembered hearing that "faith that can be destroyed by suffering is not real faith." I prayed for more faith.

"I guess I've become a real missionary now," I thought to myself, while I continued retching.

The sickness continued and I didn't participate in the eye clinic for the two days. I had never missed a day doing clinics before. Even when I was sick, I pushed through it. I remember once on a trip to Peru I would run to the outhouse, vomit, wait a couple of minutes and return to see patients. I repeated that process many times that day, but I never missed any of our clinics until this day.

On the evening of the second day, some of the doctors on the team decided to take me to the hospital.

I've toured some of the hospitals in Nicaragua and remember thinking I would never go there. One of them had numerous windows broken and, everywhere, pigeons were flying all around inside, even in the patients' rooms. Black mold grew everywhere. Broken toilets overflowed all over the floors. These medical centers just are not the clean, sterile places that we are accustomed to in the States..

Upon our arrival, we were asked if we had money and my friends said, "Yes." So even though the waiting room was filled, they immediately put us at the front of the line.

We passed a crying little boy whose arm was obviously broken, and I wondered how long he had been waiting.

The exam room floor was covered in blood, and I wondered if they had just had someone in there who had been shot or stabbed. There was blood on the table they had me sit on. They took some vitals.

"You are very dehydrated," the doctor said. "You need some IV fluids."

The doctor sent my friends out to a drugstore to purchase an IV needle to replace the one they were going to use on me. While they were gone, a nurse came in with a large needle in her hand. There was no syringe—she just had the needle which looked like a ten-penny nail.

"I am going to take some blood from you."

She straightened out my arm and, without any antiseptic wiping, she jabbed the needle into a vein. I don't know why I didn't pass out. She then turned my arm over and held a test tube underneath it. A small fountain of blood gushed into the tube, overflowed onto her gloveless hand, and began to spill onto the floor. This added to the mosaic of blood that was already there probably from all the others she had impaled. I thought perhaps I might need stitches to close the hole left by the needle. (Ok perhaps that's a slight exaggeration.)

The doctor returned a little while later and she had a much smaller IV needle in her hand. It wasn't in a wrapper. I was uncertain if it was sterile or not.

"Is it clean?" I asked.

"Yes," she said after wiping it with a Kleenex.

They started giving me fluids and I began to shiver as the liquid had been stored in a refrigerator. I received three bags of fluids. When those were finished, she brought in what looked like a milkshake.

"Mr. Bryan, if you can keep this down without vomiting, I can let you go home." She then left the room.

I'm positive it was a milkshake made from fish guts. One sip of it and I wanted to vomit all over again.

My friends returned from the pharmacy run and one of them was allowed to come back into my room.

"Quick, go into the restroom down the hall and dump this shake into the toilet. Then bring me back the empty cup," I said.

Thank the Lord, he did it.

When the doctor came back, she was astonished that I had consumed all of the contents of the container without vomiting and decided she could discharge me. The entire visit to the emergency room, the IVs, and the fish gut milkshake only cost $75.00.

The next day I started to feel a bit better, so I rejoined the team and saw patients for the rest of the trip.

When I returned home, I was still having a lot of stomach pain, so I went to my doctor who ordered a series of medical tests.

"You have diverticulitis," he told me." If you would just stop traveling for a few years all these gut issues will heal themselves. "

"That's never going to be a possibility," I told him.

Chapter Forty-Eight
TELL ME MORE

In the southeast corner of Ecuador, a lot of men work in mines that are hundreds of feet below ground. There the air is unbearably hot and polluted with toxic dust. They work long shifts for little pay. It is grueling labor.

One of those miners showed up at an eye and medical clinic we were holding near his worksite. He waited for a long time before he was seen, but eventually, he received his first pair of prescription eyeglasses.

Afterward, we began to chat. He was about sixty years old and very thin. His leathered face was heavily lined with fatigue. He admitted to me that after work he often drank until he passed out. His life was difficult, and his drinking gave him brief escapes.

"Those glasses you have just received are a gift from Jesus," I told him. Then I asked, "Have you ever heard about how much Jesus loves you?"

"No, I don't know anything at all about someone named Jesus."

He agreed to listen to me as I began to tell him about how much Jesus did love him. When I mentioned to him that Jesus was willing to die so that his sins could be forgiven, he interrupted me.

"My sins can be forgiven?" he questioned through our translator.

"I never knew that," he said. He looked as if a great weight had been lifted off his back. Then he spoke words that I will never forget.

"These words that you are telling me are making my heart leap with joy. Tell me more, tell me more!"

We spoke for a while longer and he desperately wanted to hear everything I could tell him about Jesus. After listening to me, he declared that for the rest of his life he would follow the teachings of the One who forgives his sins.

"I have never heard of the love and forgiveness of Jesus before. In this area, there is only witchcraft."

He had been taught that he would die and forever suffer because of his sins there was no redemption for him. No wonder he drank so much. The words I shared with him now gave him hope.

"Tomorrow, I am going to invite all of my friends to come and hear what you have just told me."

It was, however, our last day in that area so I introduced him to the pastor who wanted to start a church there. The pastor agreed to meet with all his friends whenever he brought them back.

This is one of the reasons God's Eyes always wants at least one pastor to be onsite with us. If I'm sharing the gospel and no one is there to nurture people afterward, I feel like I'm delivering a newborn baby and then leaving it a few days later without food or drink. Someone must be there to care for the infant believer, or their faith will die.

Some people, like this miner, become believers in a short or "sudden" period, however, for some, it is a long process. No matter the time length, new believers need to be turned over to someone who will teach and disciple them. If there will be no one there to love on them after we leave, then perhaps we should not even be going. What good is it to deliver a baby and abandon it?'

Chapter Forty-Nine
THE MAYOR'S GREEDY WIFE

God's Eyes has been to Honduras many times and one day we were holding an eye clinic in an isolated little school building somewhere in the north-central part of the country. Our entire eye team was sick that day with intestinal problems, but we all plugged along as best we could.

That afternoon after we had taken a short break for lunch, a well-dressed lady showed up with five of her friends. They walked to the front of the line and demanded to be seen next. She told me she was the wife of the mayor in that region, and they had driven over an hour from a large city to come and get free eyeglasses. I was told that I should let them be next.

That never sits well with me. Why should I have to wait on a lady and five of her friends when they could easily afford to buy eyeglasses in the city they were from? Even if I could help them, why should they get to be next? There were so many poor people who had been standing outside in the blazing sun for hours waiting to be seen before *these* ladies arrived. I wanted to speak out about it but wisely decided to say nothing.

I did as I was told, and I helped all of the ladies. I would have preferred to give them a piece of my mind and belittle them for being so greedy and for thinking they were far superior to everyone else who was there. I managed a fake smile and put up with all their fussing.

When I gave them their new prescription eyeglasses, some of them complained and said they didn't like the color of the frame I had given them, so I had to remake them. Some of the others didn't like the sunglasses I gave them, and they went through all my inventory so they could choose the ones they wanted for themselves. A few of them wanted several pairs for themselves instead of just one. Almost all of them wanted additional sunglasses and reading glasses for all the members of their families and their friends. They took up over two hours of my afternoon before they left with purses filled with prescription glasses, sunglasses, and reading glasses.

That time should have been allotted to helping the poor. I was about to explode, but I continued to mask my actual feelings. My wife said that towards the end of that day I was no longer my normal, happy self.

That night as I lay in bed, I was praying and asking Father to bless all those women. To bless them with a brick upside their heads.

"Certainly, there must be, or at least should be, some Old Testament scripture to justify that," I not so jokingly thought to myself.

They had been so rude and greedy. However, Father once again had a lesson for me to learn.

"If you are going to become a good servant, then you should cheerfully wait upon anyone I send your way."

"Damn!" I quietly thought. I knew I needed to repent for wanting them to receive retribution. Convicted, I lowered my head and prayed.

"I am very sorry, Father, and I promise from now on I will gladly try to serve anyone who shows up at God's Eyes clinics, no matter who they are, even if they are rude and undeserving.

In both the books of Luke and Matthew says, "I tell you, love your enemies, bless those who curse you, do good to those who hate you, and pray for those who mistreat you and persecute you."

These ladies were not my enemies, nor did they hate me, or curse me. Still, I didn't want to love them. I had so much to learn.

Jenn and me working in a squatter's village in the Peruvian desert.

Denny Debner and Rick Smith examining patients high in the remote mountains of Honduras.

THEY SHALL SEE GOD

A FEW DAYS LATER WE WERE DOING OUR LAST EYE clinic on that trip. We were about a two-hour drive from the village those ladies were from. We got word from someone that the mayor, whose wife barged in line at our previous clinic—who I had begrudgingly helped—requested that we shut down our last clinic for the entire afternoon. The mayor wanted us to drive to his office and see him.

Once more I was upset. Why should we stop helping the poor and drive hours out of our way just to see him? I knew that he was going to parade us around town telling all the people how he had arranged for us to come to help the people of that region. He would lie and declare that this had been all his doing and that the people should vote for him because of the great things he had made happen for the region. He had, however, nothing at all to do with us being in that region of Honduras. This happened to me on several other occasions in other countries. There was no way I wanted to stop seeing patients so that some greedy mayor could take credit for what we do in order to win his next election. I had already used up way too much time on his wife and her friends a few days before.

However, the leaders of the group I was serving with said that we needed to go. We packed up our supplies and had to turn away lots of people who really needed our help. Instead, we drove over an hour away to the mayor's office. When we got there, he invited us into a large room he had all decked out. It was there I was sure he would invite all the townspeople and boast about how much he does for them.

But that's not what happened. He threw a private celebration just to honor us! He said we had helped his wife and her friends earlier in the week and he wanted to thank us. He had arranged for some local children to dress up in traditional costumes and sing and dance for us. He offered us refreshments and he made all of us honorary citizens of his town. He had fancy certificates printed up for each of us. Each one had our names printed on them.

He told the local missionary that from now on she would have full cooperation from his office. If she ever needed anything she should be sure to contact him. He gave her a special honor and even had a fancy large wooden plaque made up for her! The rest of the afternoon was a celebration focusing on us.

HERE IS WHAT FATHER TAUGHT ME. I AM TO LOVE those I encounter whether they hate me, curse me or mistreat me, or even if they just waste my time and jump to the head of the line to use me for their gain. Father wants me to love them as he does.

1 Corinthians 13 says it all:

"If I speak in the tongues of men or of angels, but do not have love, I am only a resounding gong or a clanging cymbal. If I have the gift of prophecy and can fathom all mysteries and all knowledge, and if I have a faith that can move mountains, but do not have love, I am nothing. If I give all I possess to the poor and give over my body to hardship that I may boast, but do not have love, I gain nothing."

SO THERE IT IS. EVERYTHING I DO COUNTS FOR nothing if I do not learn to love like Father. His love is so completely different from mine. His love is patient and kind. *His* love never fails. And that is what He wants my love to look like.

I had unfairly judged this mayor's actions. His heart was good. He knew better than anyone that his wife was a difficult lady, and he was grateful for the way I treated her and her friends. I wanted justice for her actions, I wanted her to get a taste of her wrongdoings. I prejudged the mayor as being bad and wanting to use us only for political gain, but he was kind, grateful, and generous. His love looked more like God's.

Once again Father showed me, with great patience, that I still had many things to learn about loving people and becoming a servant of His.

Chapter Fifty
MORE SHELVING

I've already told you about how Father provided a larger headquarters for us and how he provided the increase in funds to pay for it. But I didn't tell you this yet: Our new warehouse was much larger than our old warehouse, which was good because we were busting out of the first one.

The new warehouse had thirty-foot-high ceilings, and much more floor space, which created the need for additional shelving. We didn't have the additional shelving, so once again I started to pray, asking God to provide more. I also asked the guys in my Friday morning men's Bible study if they would pray about it with me.

A day or so later I received a call from one of the guys in my Bible study.

"You need to call this number right now! A guy has warehouse shelves that he wants to get rid of today!"

I called the fellow and he said that "Yes" he did have shelving stored in a warehouse. He had just purchased a Staples office supply store and replaced all the original warehouse shelving with new shelving. He had plans to use all the original shelving for something else, but then he no longer needed it because he decided to move to Las Vegas. He said he was going to sell the shelving to a scrap metal dealer that day. He told me to come over right away!

I drove over to his warehouse immediately. There he had lots of heavy-duty warehouse shelving easily worth many thousands of dollars. He offered to give it all to me for free. There was just one problem. I had no place to store it. I wasn't able to move into our new warehouse for two months and my current warehouse had absolutely no room left in it at all.

"I want it but we have no place to put it."

He called me back later and said, "I called the scrap metal dealer and told him not to come. My friend, who I rent this warehouse from, said you can take over my lease temporarily until you move. That way you won't have to move all the shelving until your new warehouse is ready."

Within a few hours, all the shelving needs for our new warehouse had been supplied at no cost to God's Eyes. We also solved the storage problem for all the newly donated shelving at the same time. When I say "we," that means God. Once again I realized that God always shows up whenever we need Him to.

Philippians 4:19 says, *"My God will supply every need of yours according to his riches in glory in Christ Jesus."*

Chapter Fifty-One
GOING TO JAIL

I have visited many jails while serving on God's Eyes trips. On one trip to Haiti, I visited the prisoners in the local jail. While I was there, I learned that these prisoners do not receive any meals unless someone "on the outside" brings them something to eat. Early one evening after the eye clinics were finished, I headed back to the jail. I donated most of the snack food I brought on my trip and gave it to the prisoners. Some of the others who came with me also gave them food. There were five men in the cell we were allowed to visit. One of the prisoners was asleep on the concrete floor in the back of the cell. Three of the prisoners eagerly ran up to the cell bars and quickly accepted the food I had brought. The fifth prisoner looked straight at me.

"No! No! No! He shouted and he backed away and cowered in the farthest corner of the cell. We ignored each other.

When I returned home, I spoke with a friend.

"Did you pray for the prisoner who backed away and didn't take any food?" my friend asked.

"Nope, I only prayed with the men who came up to the bars, " I replied.

LATER THAT NIGHT THE LORD SHOWED ME HOW I missed out on another opportunity He had provided for me.

"The man who ran away from you does not believe in me. Who is going to share with him how much my Son loves him and what He did for him if you don't?" Father asked me.

I THINK IT WAS SAINT FRANCIS OF ASSISI WHO WAS quoted as saying "Preach the Gospel at all times and when necessary, use words." That day I realized *IT IS* necessary for us to use words.

LOOKING BACK ON THAT DAY, I ENDED UP DOING something good, but I missed out on doing something great which would have been doing what Father had intended for me to do. I was to tell people what Jesus has done for them, not just feed them. If we don't stay in Father's presence, we will miss out on doing the greater things that God has planned for us to do. We will only end up doing "good things" not "God things."

Chapter Fifty-Two
$21.57

The phone rang at God's Eyes headquarters. A man I did not know was calling me from two towns away. He wondered if I would be willing to come to a men's ROMEO group from his church. ROMEO is an acronym for Retired Old Men Eating Out. About thirty men from his church met for around an hour or so every Wednesday at a local Chinese restaurant for lunch. He was hoping I'd come and talk to them from 12:30 to 1:00 about God's Eyes. He said they would buy me lunch. How could I ever say no to free food?

I arrived a little before noon as instructed. The Chinese restaurant they all assembled at, held an all-you-could-eat buffet luncheon on Wednesdays and everyone there, including me, grabbed a plate of food. While we were eating, the man who invited me facilitated a church business meeting of some sort and finished talking around 12:15 pm. He turned to me.

"Would you like to talk for an extra fifteen minutes?"

"Sure," I readily agreed, I pushed my plate aside and stood up, and walked up to the podium.

"Hello guys, my name is Bryan Kaiser, and I started a nonprofit organization called God's Eyes."

As soon as I introduced myself, a man in the back of the restaurant hollered out:

"Sit down, it ain't 12:30 yet!"

"Yeah, we're still eating," another man shouted.

I wanted to explain that their leader just invited me to start speaking early, instead, I apologized and sat back down.

AT EXACTLY 12:30 SHARP I WALKED BACK UP TO THE podium and started my talk. I spoke for a while as I kept a sharp look at my watch. When it was nearly 1 p.m. I paused. I knew this was a tough crowd who all appeared to follow rules to the T, so I said,

"I'll just stop here as it's almost 1 p.m." I thanked them for having me.

As I was about to sit back down, someone in the room spoke up.

"I want to hear more."

"Well, it's already one o'clock," I answered him, "I'm supposed to stop talking."

"Keep talking. We ain't got nowhere to go," said the man who had told me to sit down earlier.

"Yeah, we're all retired. Talk as long as you want," another confirmed.

Apparently, I could talk all day as long as I didn't start before 12:30. So I told some more stories and decided to quit after I had spoken for a total of an hour. When I finished, a man stood up.

"I propose that we take up a collection for this fine young man."

"I second that motion," said another.

"Is that OK with you, Bryan?" the group leader asked me.

This had never happened to me before when I had shared about God's Eyes in other places. I responded with my usual reply when people ask me about donations.

"You can do whatever God is telling you to do," I replied.

He polled the group and the motion passed. As I was packing up my supplies, they took up a collection for me. A few minutes later their leader came over and thanked me for being there. He handed me an envelope saying the money they collected was inside.

Back at God's Eyes, I opened that envelope. Those thirty-plus men had collected $21.57. An average of about 70 cents per person.

"Wow, I really must have impressed them," I thought. Then, I began to laugh.

I laughed for two reasons. First, because I knew this would make a funny story, and second because I felt that this was probably not the end of the story.

THREE MONTHS LATER I RECEIVED ANOTHER PHONE call. This time from another lady I had never met.

"My church is considering doing a month-long fundraiser for God's Eyes. Would you be willing to come and talk to our church finance team?

I felt somewhat honored as I had never attended her church in my life.

"OK," I agreed.

The following week I met with their finance team. They confirmed they liked what God's Eyes was doing and they wanted to help us out.

"What kind of fundraisers have you done in the past?" they asked.

"We don't do fundraisers," I said.

"What kind of a fundraiser do you think we could do for you?"

"I have no clue. We have never raised funds of any kind. People just send us money," I told them. "But you guys can do whatever Father wants you to do," I said, and I left.

A week or two went by and they called me.

"How much does it cost to make a new pair of prescription eyeglasses for someone?"

"An average cost is about $13 a pair and that includes the costs of getting the glasses to whatever country the person lives in and everything else involved in actually placing them onto the person's face."

"Can you supply us with 1100 soft cloth eyeglass cases?"

"Yes."

"Bryan, this is what we feel we are supposed to do. We're going to put an eyeglass case in every bulletin and ask everyone to buy a pair of new glasses by putting $13 in the eyeglass case."

"Ok, if that's what Father is telling you to do, then I will bring the eyeglass cases to you."

And that's exactly what they did. Five weeks later I heard from the lady who first contacted me from that church.

"We've finished our fundraiser. Can I come by and drop off the check?" she asked.

"Sure," I said. Later that day she stopped by.

"Before you open this envelope, I want you to know something. We've raised more money for this fundraiser than we have ever raised for any other fundraiser." It turned out to be enough to cover the rent at God's Eyes headquarters for several months.

"Thank you, this is awesome. But I have a question for you. How did you ever hear about me and God's Eyes?"

"Four months ago, you were at a luncheon, and you spoke to my husband's ROMEO group," she answered. He came home that day in tears and said I should have heard the stories you told. I figured that anyone who can move my husband to tears is worthy of raising money for."

I silently chuckled as I gazed upward towards the sky. I knew there was more to the story than the $21.57 I received the day I first spoke to the ROMEO group.

⌒⌒

Chapter Fifty-Three
THE GRADUATION MONEY

When our youngest daughter graduated from high school, my wife wanted to throw her a graduation party. It gave her a great excuse to invite family members from all over the country to our house. She spent $200 on food, party decorations, and cake. At one point in my life, spending $200 would have been a minor expense. At that time, however, after years of living on just my wife's income and being frugal, I thought that this was a rather significant amount for us to spend. To help me with my attitude, my wife asserted that it would be the only time our daughter would ever graduate from high school, and she was the last of our three children who was going to do that. So, we threw her a simple, but nice, party.

The following Sunday I was getting ready to go to church and I had on my blue jeans, flip-flops, and a comfortable shirt.

"You're not actually going to church dressed like that are you?" she said with a look of, you've got to be kidding me on her face.

"I'm a missionary now and missionaries don't need to dress to impress anyone."

"I agree, but I think you are perhaps taking this missionary dress thing a bit too far. I think you at least need to wear shoes and maybe consider putting a sports jacket on."

So I went to my closet, changed shoes, grabbed a sports coat, and put it on. But then I thought to myself, "Nah, forget it. I'm not going to wear this," and I hung it back up.

WHEN I DID THAT, I NOTICED THERE WAS SOMETHING in the front pocket of the blazer. I reached in the pocket and found two new one-hundred-dollar bills.

I know for sure I hadn't put any money in there, but I guessed maybe the last time I wore this jacket at a speaking event perhaps someone had anonymously slipped the money into my jacket pocket. Maybe something even crazier happened. Maybe God just made the money appear. Whatever the case, I felt God was giving us the money back that we spent on our daughter's graduation party. I was happy.

We left for church immediately after I discovered that money. In our church, there is a coffee bar area where you can sit down and enjoy a cup of coffee before or after the services. I sat down in the lounge area and was enjoying a cup of cappuccino.

A man came and sat down with me, and we began talking. He thanked me for a talk I had given the weekend before at a men's gathering.

"I need to learn to live by faith more. I've thought about it ever since hearing you talk about doing that at the men's breakfast meeting."

He continued, "Recently I quit my job that paid quite well. I did that so I could help my wife start up her new insurance business, but things haven't turned out as we had hoped. We're now falling behind on bills and times are becoming very difficult financially for us."

When he said that I felt like Father wanted me to give him the $200 I had found only thirty minutes earlier. I opened my wallet in front of him and pulled out the two one-hundred-dollar bills.

"It's strange, but I just found this money in one of my sports coat's pockets just a little while ago. It was the same amount we spent last weekend on my daughter's graduation party."

I handed the bills to him.

"I believe that Father wants me to give these to you."

"No, no, no! I can't take money from a missionary."

"But it's not from me, it's from Father and I'm fairly certain that this is why He gave me the money in the first place."

He could not believe it.

"I can't believe a missionary is giving me money!"

He thanked me over and over.

"You're thanking the wrong person," I said as I left to enter the sanctuary leaving him alone in the coffee lounge with $200 in his hands. What I didn't know, until three months later, was that he never stayed for the church service. He was just so shocked that he went home. When he got there, he told his wife the whole story about how he got $200.

"What do you think we need to do with this money?" he asked her.

She told him that Verizon was shutting off their cell phones if they did not pay them $200 by noon that day.

"Do you think we can make it to a Verizon store by then?

"If we leave right now, I think we can."

They flew out the door, made it to Verizon, and their phones were never turned off. They only had cell phones at their business, so if those phones had been cut off, they would have had to close.

After that day things began to improve for them and today, they are doing just fine.

That all happened on a Sunday. Four days later on Thursday, a man walked into our headquarters at God's Eyes. He sat down at the conference table. He pulled out his checkbook and began writing. He made out a check, not to God's Eyes, but to me personally for … you probably have guessed it … $200! I felt like God had just replaced the money He had me give away.

It's wonderful how Father works.

"Seek first His kingdom and its righteousness and all these things shall be added unto you." Matthew 6:33

ᴖᴖ

Chapter Fifty-Four
STORIES OF GIVING

According to the *Christian Science Monitor*, Americans recently have spent more money buying Halloween costumes for their pets than the amount given to missions to reach the lost. This statement makes the following even more inspiring to me. Here are just a few of the many stories I have regarding donations.

* * *

A LADY I MET AT A MISSION'S WEEK CHURCH EVENT was the mother of a small boy around nine or ten years old. She is not well off financially, but she decided to donate enough money to us every month. She donated enough money so that one poor person in the world could receive sight. Of all the donations that come in every month, hers is the smallest, but to me, it is one of the greatest. Every time her check arrives it makes me smile. When you have faith, it changes how you live … and how you give.

When I returned to that mission week at her church the following year, her young son came up and gave me two plastic bags filled with coins. He told me that he had saved all his change for the entire year, and he wanted to give it all to God's Eyes so that children in other countries could see. When I returned to my office, I counted both bags of coins. There was over $40 worth of pennies, nickels, dimes, and quarters. I donated an equal amount of money so that I could keep all that change on display. I poured those coins into a tray, which sits on my credenza to this day. Every time I look at that tray full of change, I think of that little boy's heart and how he already has the correct mindset about giving.

* * *

A LADY, I NEVER HEARD OF OR MET, ONCE SENT God's Eyes a contribution. Her phone number was on the check, so I called her to thank her. I asked her how she heard about us. She said she had awakened one morning and put on her eyeglasses. She realized how wonderful it was to see everything clearly. She had poor uncorrected vision, so she had worn eyeglasses to correct her sight ever since she was a little girl. She was so grateful that she decided she wanted to buy a pair of eyeglasses for someone. She searched "eyeglasses for poor people" on the internet. Even though God's Eyes was on about page 84 on google search, somehow our name popped up on her screen and she sent us a check. It was enough money to buy several pairs of eyeglasses for others.

* * *

A COUPLE WE KNOW HAD A GARAGE SALE. THEY wanted to donate all the proceeds to God's Eyes. It rained violently the entire weekend of the garage sale. In fact, that weekend set a record for the wettest weekend in Georgia for the entire year. Despite the weather, God sent people out in the rain for bargains, and they raised over $1,100 for us.

* * *

AN EYE DOCTOR FROM A SMALL TOWN HEARD ABOUT us and called us. He had traveled to third-world countries on mission trips and had seen firsthand the incredible need for eye care. He cares about those who cannot see, so he donated over 1,000 new prescription lenses to us.

* * *

ONE DAY I WENT TO THE MAILBOX AND OPENED A letter containing a check. It was from a man I did not know. He sent us a check for $4,050. His phone number was on the check, so I called him up and thanked him for such a generous donation.

"How did you learn about us?" I asked.

"Let me tell you a story, he said," I inherited some money, so I wanted to share some of it with someone who needed help. I asked a good friend of mine, 'If you could help any group in the world, who would you help?' He said, 'God's Eyes.' A few days later, I asked a second friend who they would help. They, too, answered, 'God's Eyes.' A couple of weeks later, I asked a third friend. He said, 'I would give money to this guy who runs God's Eyes.' Finally, I asked a fourth friend of mine who they would help, and they answered, 'God's Eyes'. I'm not completely sure I know what you actually do, but I figured after four people said they would help God's Eyes that God was probably trying to tell me something, so I sent you a check."

* * *

A COUPLE SOLD THEIR HOME. THEY CARE DEEPLY about those who are poor and lack supplies. They learned how to pour out love and they had spent their lives doing that. Instead of keeping the money from the sale of their house for retirement, they donated it to God's Eyes, and we were able to give the gift of sight to over 10,000 people.

* * *

THEY SHALL SEE GOD

A LOT OF PETS WOULD HAVE BEEN DISAPPOINTED by these people because they didn't spend their money on animal Halloween costumes. Instead, these people and hundreds of more, have demonstrated what Father meant when he taught us the following verse:

Philippians 2:3 says,

"Instead of being motivated by selfish ambition or vanity, each of you should, in humility, be moved to treat one another as more important than yourself."

Chapter Fifty-Five
LUNCH AT WENDY'S

At the God's Eyes office one day I was busy packing up all the supplies I needed to send out. As usual, I kept questioning whether I had enough lenses made. I decided we could use some more so I started edging more lenses, which put me even farther behind in packing. I worked through lunch, and when it was past 4 p.m. I was hungry. I decided to take a break and run out to get something to eat.

At a nearby shopping center, there were several choices of places to eat including some fast-food restaurants. I looked in my wallet and saw that I had a $10 bill and two $1 bills. I decided I would go through Wendy's drive-through and order off the dollar menu and save my $10 bill for later.

I ordered a small hamburger and the value fries which came to $2.10 with tax. I gave the girl at the window my two $1 bills.

"Just a minute. I'll get you the ten cents." I knew I could find the ten cents somewhere in my car. I always have lots of loose change floating around in my car.

That day, however, even after spending five minutes looking high and low, I couldn't find one single penny in change. I shunned the thought of having to break a $10 bill just to pay ten cents. But I had no choice. I gave the cashier my ten.

"Just take it out of this," I sadly said.

To my delight, she handed it back to me and said not to worry about it, that she would pay the ten cents herself. This made me happy, but as I was putting the ten back into my wallet, I felt Father say something.

"Give it to her as a tip."

Well, I wanted to have a conversation with Him about that, and it went something along these lines.

"God, you don't tip the people working at a fast-food restaurant and even if you did, you wouldn't tip them $10 on a $2 order. That would be stupid."

At least that was what I wanted to tell Him, but by that time in my life, I had learned that you can never win an argument with Father. So, unenthusiastically, I handed the $10 back to her.

"This is for you," I said as I forced a smile upon my face.

You would have thought that I had just given her a million dollars. She was smiling from ear to ear. She was ecstatic and thanked me many times.

"No, you need to thank God because He wanted you to have it." If I'm being completely honest, I wanted to keep it for myself.

As I drove away, I complained, to no one, that my mini-burger and fries were now cold from having spent so much time looking for a dime. As I drove out of the parking lot, I passed an Outback Steakhouse.

"For the $12 I just spent I could have eaten lunch there and had a nice steak sandwich with delicious sides. Just like I used to do when I was making money while working," I thought to myself.

Again, I heard Father speaking.

"Bryan, that girl gave you ten cents of her own money. Then I asked you to give her $10 of yours. I just used you to be a 'hundredfold blessing' to someone."

Wow! As soon as I heard that, my attitude immediately changed. I no longer was complaining about my cold food or how much I spent. I just got to take part in a hundredfold blessing to someone and that made me feel great.

I WORKED UNTIL 7 P.M. THAT NIGHT AND DROVE home. I went to my mailbox and inside was a check for $1,000. It was one hundred times the $10 I had given away earlier in the day.

I REALIZED I HAD TO MAKE A CHOICE EARLIER THAT day. It was whether I would obey what Father had asked me to do. I couldn't help but believe that if I had not been obedient and given that young girl $10, there would not have been $1,000 in my mailbox that evening. I was learning that God will oftentimes reward obedience.

"Do all that I command, and good things will happen to you." (Jeremiah 7:23)

＊

Chapter Fifty-Six
MAKE MORE PIES

E arly on in my journey of becoming who Father wanted me to be, I attended
a missionary conference that had a seminar titled, "How to Raise Support
from Churches." I was already committed to letting Father fund our ministry,
but I thought I would amuse myself and listen to expert advice on this matter.

The man speaking was the head of the benevolence and missionary support
programs that his megachurch offered. In short, he taught that most churches
have a financial pie chart of their church budgets. On that chart, there is usually
a very small slice dedicated to mission and benevolence work. He went on
about how many groups want a bite out of that small piece of the pie. Every
year he received numerous requests for funding by new mission groups and
increased support requests from groups they were already funding.

At best he said they might have room to add one new ministry. If they
had had a phenomenally generous year of giving, the previous year, perhaps
they would consider adding two more groups to their list of beneficiaries.

He began to elaborate by saying, "To be added to the list of possible
candidates, your missionary organization must have a professionally prepared
DVD telling me all about your ministry. That DVD must state all the accomplishments of your ministry including previous years and all future ideas for
growth and development. In the DVD you must state the specific projects that
require funding and the exact amount of support needed. Also, to be included

are detailed plans of how the money is going to be spent. If you don't do this, there is no way I will even consider your request."

"Quite honestly, I just throw most letters asking for support into the garbage can without even reading them. If you take the time and have prepared a DVD, I might consider watching it. The fact of the matter is most churches have already decided who they are going to support from the small piece of the pie dedicated to missions."

He closed by stating, "Realistically, it is extremely hard to raise support through churches."

I thought to myself how silly all of this sounded. My God wasn't worried about dividing up a small piece of pie for everyone. The God I knew did things like these:

In Exodus 16:4, God rained down bread from Heaven to feed his people.

John 2:7-9 Jesus turned water into wine when the wine they had for a wedding ran out.

In Matthew 14 and John 5 there is a story that explains how five loaves of bread and two fish were multiplied to feed over 5,000 people. Then in Matthew 15, Jesus took seven loaves of bread and the fish he was given and fed 4,000 people with it.

In 1 Kings 17, God used ravens to deliver bread and meat to Elijah in the morning and the evening.

In Exodus 17, God had Moses strike the rock in the desert and water flowed out of it.

In 2 Kings 4, God used twenty loaves of bread and some grain to feed over 100 men. In this story and others, not only did everyone have enough to eat, but there were plenty of leftovers.

THAT "EXPERT" TAUGHT US THAT CHURCHES ARE only able to help a few ministries a little bit. I've grown to realize that churches and ministries that have faith will see Father supply all their needs and even extra for others. My God isn't worried about having to divide up a small piece of the financial pie, He just makes more pies!

Chapter Fifty-Seven
THE ANNUAL REPORT

A few years after starting God's Eyes, in the middle of December, I decided to go on a ten-day fast. It wasn't a complete fast, but I decided to only eat fruits and vegetables. During that time, I was praying Psalm 51:10 *"Create a clean heart in me, O God, and renew a faithful spirit within me."*

Since it was toward the end of the year I thought I would send out a year-end report for God's Eyes. We did not usually send out monthly or even quarterly newsletters. None of our donors had heard anything about what we did all year. I was feeling a responsibility to report on what we did with their donations that year.

I started to write an annual report. As I wrote I was also praying.

"What are you doing?" Father questioned.

"I'm writing the end of the year report!" I said pridefully.

"Why are you doing that?" He asked.

"Well, no one has heard from us all year and I feel some sort of fiduciary responsibility to our donors so I'm letting them know what I did this year. It's been such an amazing year. This year we've handed out more eyeglasses than the previous three years combined!"

"No, why are you really doing it?" He asked again.

I thought briefly and I realized I had worded my last answer incorrectly.

God's Eyes Team preparing to ship 325,000 lenses to El Salvador

A standard God's Eyes clinic setup in a small village in Panama

"I'm doing it because I want everyone to know what YOU have done, Lord!" This time I felt positive that I got the answer right.

"No, why are you really doing that?"

Hmmm, I was sure that my last answer was correct, but I began to ponder why I might honestly be writing the newsletter. After several minutes I answered.

"You wouldn't mean I'm doing it because it's the end of the year and that people give more money in December than nearly all other months combined? Perhaps if I send out a newsletter letting everyone know of the great works that You are doing, they might send some of their donations our way to sneak in another tax deduction? Could that be why I'm doing this?"

"Oh, so you're in charge of raising money now?" Father replied.

Those words stung. If I was fully honest, raising end-of-year funds was exactly what I had hoped to accomplish. Foolishly I was trying to convince myself that it was to report on what Father did. I knew He was right. I was trying to help Him bring in more money.

I hung my head and repented. I had been asking God to create in me a clean heart during my fast and he was showing me a dirty spot.

If we have dirty hearts, we ruin our ability to follow Father's teachings.

"I'm so sorry Lord. What should I do?"

"Don't send out the letter until January when no one will have any money leftover from Christmas and they will have no need to donate until the end of the next year." I secretly disagreed but kept my thoughts to myself, but I suppose the Lord knew them anyway. I wanted to have the following conversation:

"Lord, World Vision just sent me a thirty-page colored catalog. They show that I can buy a goat for a poor family. Or that I can buy Bibles for people to read, or bags of rice or chickens so a family can eat. I can send a child to school and buy them school uniforms. I can buy food, clothing, cows, all types of supplies, and hundreds of different items. Heck, I can even buy a family a house! Don't you know, Lord, that World Vision is the most successful Christian nonprofit group with an annual budget of 2.5 BILLION dollars? If they're sending out a end of the year newsletter that will raise funds, shouldn't

God's Eyes follow the lead of one of the most successful non-profit ministries? Shouldn't we take advantage of this season of giving?"

I knew, however, that He would have told me to listen to Him and not my own worldly logic, so I never had that conversation.

C.S. Lewis once said, "When you argue against Him you are arguing against the very power that makes you able to argue at all; it is like cutting off the branch you are sitting on."

I had already learned that you can never win an argument with Father anyway, so what would be the point. Therefore, when Father told me not to write the letter until January, I conceded my argument and just said, "OK," but my heart and head still carried a stubborn stain. Somewhere in a far corner of my mind, I believed that not sending out the letter was a lost opportunity.

Surprisingly, without any updates from us as to what we did for an entire year, we received more money that December than ever before. I once again learned that I don't need to help Father supply for His ministry. He is more than capable of doing that alone. Once again, I learned that Father delights in our obedience. In the book of Samuel, it says obedience is even more important than sacrifice.

Around the middle of January, I began to rewrite the previous year-end report and was once again fasting and praying as I wrote it.

I heard Father asking me another question.

"What are you doing now, Bryan?" Here we go again I thought, but this time I felt confident that I had the correct response.

"I'm writing the year-end newsletter for last year as you told me to and Lord, I have no hidden agendas in my heart this time. You blessed us so much with donations in December and I am not expecting even a penny from this report. I just want to tell everyone what You did last year."

"Why are you really writing the letter?" He asked again.

"I told You why. I am doing it to let everyone know what *You've* done with your ministry of God's Eyes."

"Why are you using numbers?" I heard.

"Well … it's to exalt You and declare your awesome accomplishments so that the donors will know how incredible You are! How else will they know how many eyeglasses God's Eyes gave out and how many people got saved at the eye clinics."

"That's not why you're doing this, Bryan! You are writing the letter because you want an *A*."

Oh my, boy did that ever hit me hard. Of course, He was right! I did want an *A*. I wanted to prove to all my friends, who said I was crazy for shutting down my businesses and taking this leap, that I was not crazy at all. I wanted to show them how successful we had become in such a short amount of time! I secretly wanted to throw a little pie in their face. Once again, in the presence of His light, He revealed a dirty blemish in my heart.

"You are right, God! I am so sorry, what should I do?"

"Write the letter without any numbers in it," He said. "It's my ministry, I know what I've done. All those eyeglasses you handed out, I provided. All the people who prayed to follow Me, I drew them in. All those numbers, Bryan, belong to Me and you shouldn't use them that way."

Deep inside I knew the reasons I wanted to use those numbers. I would look praiseworthy as a leader and prove that God's Eyes is worthy and deserving of receiving ongoing donations. I think perhaps many ministries do that. The better the numbers we have, the better the chance our ministry will continue to be funded and survive. Survival of the ministry can be a hidden motive for desiring achievement. We sometimes use Father's numbers for our own exaltation, and we are robbing Him of the glory only He deserves.

I did as He requested, I wrote the letter without using numbers and wrote the following instead.

"I could foolishly boast about the number of eyeglasses we dispensed this past year and the number of people who opened the gift of forgiveness and made commitments to follow His teachings. But Father provided all the people we saw with new eyeglasses, and it was Him alone who drew people into His kingdom."

It was all Him and none of me. Period!

After I had finished writing the letter Father asked me,

"Do you want to know what your goals are for God's Eyes this year?"

"Yes, I shouted! You see, I love working with goals! I'm good at obtaining them. That's how I succeeded in business. I set goals every year and I did whatever was necessary to obtain them."

I was so excited that Father was going to give me specific goals that I pulled out a new notebook and wrote "Goals for this Year" on the cover.

BUT BEFORE I GET TO WHAT HE SAID, I WANT TO share a theory in economics called the "Goodhart Law." It can be applied to many areas in life. Of course, Father is aware of it. It states that "When a measure becomes a target, it ceases to be a good measure." In order to achieve a set target, individuals may take action to achieve the target. This can undermine the true purpose that setting the target was meant to achieve.

If, for example, I set a goal of handing out 10,000,000 glasses, I might reach that impressive goal. However, I could miss the true cause of the goal which had nothing to do with the number of glasses dispensed. Rather we are to hold eye clinics so we can share the love that Father has for people.

"I'M READY, LORD. WHAT ARE MY GOALS FOR GOD'S Eyes this year?"

"You have none," He said. "It's my ministry and not yours. Your only goal is to become a better servant to me."

God does not need me to help him succeed. He does not need me to increase any numbers. He does not need me to obtain His goals. My only goal was to be a better servant.

EVERY YEAR THE MOST COMMON QUESTIONS I'M asked are "How many eyeglasses have you handed out?" and "What is the total number of people who have been saved through God's Eyes clinics?"

After learning the lesson that those numbers belong only to Father, I used to answer those questions by just saying, "A lot."

I realized that if we are using His numbers it exalts us or the ministries we run, and it robs Father of the glory that only He deserves.

I answered by saying, "A lot," for many years, until one day Father told me He wanted to correct me. He said the response, *A lot,* still implies a very large number, so I was still boasting by answering that way.

"How should I answer those questions then?" I asked Him.

He told me what my response should be.

"The correct answer to how many people have we helped and how many have been saved at God's Eyes clinics is simply, 'Not enough.'"

Chapter Fifty-Eight
EXTRAORDINARY

Once I started going on these mission trips, it seemed like my life was spent in a better way as I helped others who were less fortunate than myself.

One time on a flight back home from a mission trip in Central America, I had booked myself an aisle seat because I prefer those. I had been upgraded by Delta because I fly so much. They gave me a window seat in a nicer part of the plane. I felt good mentally, as I usually do right after finishing a trip.

As I relaxed on the flight, I placed my head against the window and stared outside. I reflected over the things that had taken place on the trip and thanked Father for everything He did. This feeling of peace and awe came over me as I realized the miracle of being able to travel around the world on a plane. I was sitting in a 175,000-pound piece of metal 35,000 feet above the ground traveling over 500 mph. At that height, you can see things as far away as 230 miles. I watched the large cargo ships in the Atlantic Ocean. They looked like small bugs swimming as I watched from the plane. Even though I had seen that a hundred times before, I marveled at the technology the Lord shared with men to make flying possible. I was filled with peace and felt grateful. As I was quietly thanking Father for this gift of flying, I heard Him asking me a question.

"Bryan, do you want to live an ordinary life or an extraordinary life?"

As I pondered that, I concluded there wasn't a right or wrong answer— I felt that Father just wanted to know which one I wanted. After a few minutes, I answered Him.

"If the decision was up to me, if you're really leaving that choice up to me, well, I guess I would choose 'extraordinary.' But how do I do that Lord?"

"The first thing you have got to do to live an extraordinary life is to learn how to pour out love."

I remembered agreeing with that immediately and I spent several minutes thinking of great people I have known and how they loved so freely and abundantly. Without the release of love, my life would never live up to its fullest potential. Nothing is more important than learning how to freely dispense love. Nothing else comes even close. Then Father said more.

"The second thing you have to do is to become teachable AND correctable."

I contemplated that as well. It seems to me that many people are teachable, but very few are willing to be corrected. I knew I should be more willing to open myself up to corrections from Father.

In many areas of my life, when Father tries to correct me, He is greeted with my resistance. Stubbornly, I believe the way I do things is the right way to do them, but frequently only because I had always done them that way. This kind of thinking blocks His ability to correct me. Change is difficult. I knew I needed to at least acknowledge the possibility that some of the things I had previously learned were not correct. This is what Father taught me that day on the plane.

As I continue to walk out this journey of faith with the leap I've taken into missionary work, Father has had to correct numerous wrong teachings that I once was convinced were right.

When I allow Him to correct me, God can turn the ordinary into the extraordinary.

∽⊙⊙

Chapter Fifty-Nine
GIVING THE BEST GIFT EVER

ONE NIGHT I HAD A DREAM.

I was in a large warehouse. I mean unbelievably large. On each side of this warehouse were shelves perhaps fifty yards deep, maybe a hundred feet tall. The warehouse went on as far as I could see. In fact, it was so long that I couldn't even see where it ended. There was a road in the middle of the warehouse dividing it into two sides. Each side of the warehouse was identical. The shelves reached high into the air. On each shelf were millions upon millions of the most beautifully wrapped gifts that you ever saw. Each one was in the same sized box. The wrapping was extravagant, and the bows and ribbons were amazing. I had never seen gifts wrapped so beautifully before and each, although the same dimensions, was wrapped differently from the others.

"What are all these gifts, Father, and who are they for?"

"Inside them is the gift of eternal life. They are for you to hand out and offer. They are beautifully wrapped because the gift inside is so very beautiful and valuable. I want you to remember that when handing them out. If the person you offer the gift to wants it, let them open it and keep what's inside. And if they don't want it, just put it back where you found it so it can be offered again another time by someone else. You can come here as often as you want, and you can take all that you can carry or load up. If you need help loading or handing them out, I will send you people who will help. Just make sure to hand them out."

THEY SHALL SEE GOD

I BELIEVE THE WAREHOUSE IN THIS DREAM IS AC-
cessible to anyone who desires to evangelize. I know there is a spiritual gift of
evangelism and I know I do not have that. I know some people make a career
as evangelists, and again I know I am not one of those. However, I have been
commanded by Father to do the work of one whether I have that gift or not.
Read 2 Timothy 4, verse 5. I think I had this dream, to remind myself and others
to hand out the gift of love that Father has prepared.

IT IS NOT UP TO ME TO FORCE ANYONE TO OPEN IT.
Not at all. However, I am supposed to offer the gift to everyone I can. Father
has also taught me that it shouldn't seem like a job, a chore, or an undesirable
task, but it ought to be my delight to hand out the gift. I should be thrilled
and enthusiastic as I offer such a beautiful and costly gift.

ONE TIME WHILE I WAS PRAYING, FATHER WAS
teaching me another lesson related to that dream.

"Bryan, think of a time when you gave a present to someone and you
thought they would love it so much you couldn't wait for them to open it."

I thought back to a time when my son was ten years old. For Christmas, I
had bought him a complete set of junior-sized golf clubs and a red-and-white
Wilson golf bag. He never asked for them, but I knew he would go crazy over
the clubs when he opened them. He would then be able to play with me when
I went golfing. He would see it as a sign of growing up. He'd get to play on a
real golf course and not just ride with me. He'd now be able to do more than
just putting the ball when we were on the greens.

I loved giving him the clubs because it now meant my son could spend time
with me doing what I enjoyed the most. I knew it would be a great bonding
experience. To this day I believe my love for the sport remains unrivaled by
anyone other than my son. There is almost nothing I enjoy more than going
golfing with him.

That Christmas after all the other presents had been opened, I brought his golf clubs out of the closet where I had hidden them. I can still remember his beaming face.

Then I thought of a couple of other times when my children received gifts from me. When my son was eighteen, we gave him an Apple MacBook Air computer. He didn't know it was coming, but Jenn and I knew he would flip out over it, and he did. When my daughter Ashley was sixteen, I bought her a convertible and couldn't wait to see how much happiness it brought her.

"OK, Father, you told me to think of some of these special moments and I've thought of these three. Why did you want me to do that?"

"When you share the story of how much my Son loves the people you are talking to, which is my gift to them, I want you to do it with the same joy, excitement, and anticipation that you had when you gave those gifts to your children. When they open my gift, watch their faces light up. My gift is even more wonderful than the ones you provided for your son and daughter. Just remember to handle it and treat it as carefully as you treated the gifts you gave to your children."

Chapter Sixty
WHAT'S BETTER?

I traveled to northern Uganda one summer where the God's Eyes team served with another amazing group named Children's Hope Chest. Our purpose there was to examine the eyes of hundreds and hundreds of orphaned children, but as often happens on our trips, many adults from nearby villages also showed up at the clinic.

During the subjective part of the exam when we asked, "Which lens is better: one or two?" the people didn't respond. They simply told me what they could see with each lens. They said, "I can see the cow," or "I can see a tree."

"Yes, I know you can see the cow! But which of these two lenses helps you see better? The first one or the second one?"

They would always repeat the same thing no matter what lens I held up: "I see the cow."

Frustrated, I told the translator:

"I know they can see the stupid cow!!! But which of these lenses do they like better?"

The translator spoke something that floored me.

"They do not understand the concept of the word 'better'" as most of them have never had the chance to choose anything in their life. The word "better" doesn't exist in their vocabulary."

For me, that was a real eye-opener (no pun intended), these people had to make do with whatever they had. Imagine living life under those conditions where choices are rarely offered. They learned to accept the hand life had dealt them. There was simply a lack of options for them and that broke my heart. Once again it was perfectly clear to me how amazingly blessed we are to live in the States where we enjoy so many choices.

ADDITIONAL HEART-CRUSHING MOMENTS HAPPEN when we frequently examine patients with eye conditions we just cannot fix at the clinic. Often these are eye problems that could be easily treated back in the States. Most of the time in the villages where we travel, these ailments go untreated and that frequently leads to very limited or no vision at all for the poor around the world.

Cataracts are one of these conditions where a simple surgery could restore good vision. However, for many, that is never going to happen in these poor remote areas. They do not have that option and they never will. This is always heartbreaking and sometimes you just cry out to the Lord on their behalf because you so deeply want to help them. To them, you are their hope, and you do not want to break their hearts by telling them you can't help them.

On one trip to Uganda, many people from our team cried out to the Lord in desperation and compassion for those who lived there. He showed up and healed many different diseases, including some eyes with cataracts. Hardships often send us running back to Father. In His presence prayers are sometimes answered in hard to believe, amazing ways.

Chapter Sixty-One
ARE YOU COMFORTABLE NOW?

I am a spoiled, North American, suburban, white, Christian, male who has spent his life enjoying comforts and standards of living that most of the world has never even heard of or will ever experience. Since entering the mission field, I've stayed in many rooms, dorms, buildings, motels, or houses that I would never have considered acceptable in my pre-missionary life. I can accept it now, but I still don't care for it. I still desire to always be comfortable.

ANYTIME I'M FORCED TO ACCEPT SOMETHING OTHER than what I'm used to, I have the propensity to complain. Instead of complaining though, I believe that Father wants all of us to learn to be content in all circumstances. (Philippians 4: 11-12) If I could ever learn how to pull that off, I think my walk would be more in line with what Father expects out of me. For me, it's been hard to shed myself of the desire for comfort. I know I have a long way to go but slowly I'm trying to live with a more accepting attitude towards discomfort.

ONCE IN ZAMBIA, I HEARD A MAN SHARING THIS story: He believed he was being called to be a missionary in the country of Chad. He was very poor and could not afford transportation, so he walked over two thousand miles to get there! Just in case you didn't know, temperatures often average over one hundred degrees in central and northern Africa. He walked through extreme heat for two thousand miles, and I complain when having to travel in various crowded, and uncomfortable modes of transportation.

So yes, every time I am crammed into a small, dilapidated vehicle of some sort, I know I should be thankful to have any kind of transportation at all. Even with lousy transportation, I don't have to walk when I travel. Only most of the time I'm not thankful. Being a missionary doesn't mean you've got this discomfort thing down pat. It doesn't even mean you're a decent character. For me, it just means I'm beginning to realize that I have no right to complain at all.

ONE TIME IN HAITI WE ARRIVED AT A MISSION BASE and there were no beds left in the dorms for us to sleep in.

"So where will we sleep?" I questioned the mission director.

"Anywhere you want to."

"You mean on the concrete?" I said with an "are you kidding me" look on my face. He then replied with something I would never forget.

"Haitians sleep on the concrete," he said soberly. "You didn't bring a sleeping bag with you?"

"No," I said as he walked past me. At the door, he turned around.

"You should have."

For the first time in my life, I realized I felt entitled. I thought if we went to a country to help people, and we are paying for the privilege to serve there, then we should at the very least be entitled to a bed.

Like a slap in the face, I had just learned another hard lesson: I'm not any better of a person than the people who live in this poor country.

ON ANOTHER OCCASION I LET CIRCUMSTANCES GET the best of me. The person who was our in-country coordinator had made arrangements for us that seemed to lack even the remotest resemblance of common sense whatsoever. I tried, at least for a while, to tolerate this coordinator's ineptness. After enduring a few days of utter frustration, I didn't hold back my feelings. I made sure to express my discontent to anyone on the trip who would listen. Before the trip was over, I had half the team complaining the same way I did. Complaining is a contagious disease.

WHEN I GOT BACK HOME FATHER ONCE AGAIN WANT-ed to teach me something. I opened my Bible and there it was front and center. I was stung by the words in Philippians 2:14: *"Do all things without grumbling or complaining."*

I had complained about nearly everything. I asked Father why everything on that trip bothered me so much and He led me to Colossians 3:2: *"Keep your mindset on things above and not on the things on earth."*

And Philippians 4:8: *"Finally, brothers, whatever is true, whatever is honorable, whatever is just, whatever is pure, whatever is lovely, whatever is commendable, if there is any excellence, if there is anything worthy of praise, think about these things.*

EVERYTHING ON THAT TRIP WAS OUTSIDE OF MY narrow North American comfort zone and efficiency desires. It all bothered me because I did none of the things Father asks us to do in those verses. I did not keep my mind on the things Father asked me to, instead I dwelt on everything that was done wrong or created an inconvenience for me. I realized how mistaken I was. Once again, I told God I was sorry, I knew His words were always right. My mind was not set on things above, rather it was set on the undesirable conditions of the trip. I allowed the unpleasant circumstances to rob me of my peace. This caused me to complain, and that is not the right thing to do. My thoughts belonged on things above and I need to become better at finding contentment in the uncomfortable.

IF I EVER LEARN TO DO WHAT THE BIBLE SUGGESTS, such as being grateful for what I have and not complaining about what I'm enduring. I will become a much more pleasant and better servant for Father. Just like He asked me to be years earlier.

Chapter Sixty-Two
CHOOSING THE RIGHT POWER

Yesterday I made a pair of eyeglasses for a friend. He thought they looked good on him. His wife thought they made him look great. I thought they looked good on him, too. It is funny how in America we are so concerned with how glasses make us look. In the past at my optical dispensaries, I sold many pairs of eyeglasses without any prescription lenses in them—only blank lenses—just because people thought they looked better or more intelligent while wearing a certain type of frame. Others chose to wear contact lenses instead of eyeglasses because they thought wearing no frames made them look better.

In poor places outside of the States where I have traveled, most poor people just want to see. When you are truly poor, you are not concerned about how glasses make you look, you just want to see clearly. I have a picture of an elderly lady in Haiti. I am guessing she is in her eighties. I made her a pair of glasses surrounded by black, thick, horn-rimmed frames. She did not care how the glasses made her look. She cared only about being able to see. There is a picture of her smiling from ear to ear while wearing that heavy bullet-proof frame for her lenses. She looks beautiful even though the glasses do not. She is content with just having the power she needs to see clearly. She only wanted what she needed and that makes her wise.

THEY SHALL SEE GOD

IN AMERICA WHEN YOU GO TO THE EYE DOCTOR TO get an exam, most practices have a technician who will do some basic pre-testing before you see the doctor. Because of this pre-testing, the doctor already knows how much power your eye requires to focus properly. After the doctor comes in, they will usually perform more tests. One of these tests involves a piece of equipment called a phoropter. This machine contains many lenses of different powers. The doctor places this machine in front of your eyes and rotates the lenses.

"Do you see better with power number 1 or number 2?" they ask.

He or she will continue to change the power of the lenses until you determine what power you say helps you see most clearly. When a patient chooses the power that confirms what the pre-testing had already determined, it's a "no-brainer." The doctor simply writes down the prescription and knows you will see things clearly.

If a patient chooses a power that is many steps different from what the pre-testing had determined was best for their eyes, it creates a dilemma. What prescription should the doctor write if the physics of light and refraction does not agree with the power the patient selects? I have seen many patients insist they see better with a power far different from what they need. When we make eyeglasses for these patients in the power they choose, it almost always results in the patient returning later and complaining that the eyeglasses aren't working out for them.

I have remade eyeglasses for some patients five or six times because they just keep choosing a power they do not need. Sometimes they want more power than they need, this is especially true of nearsighted people, and yet other times some choose a power far much less than what their eyes require.

SIMILARLY, IT SEEMS OUR HEAVENLY FATHER KNOWS what we need before we even ask Him. If we choose the correct amount of power that God knows we need ... It's again a no-brainer and we will see the situations in our lives the way God intended us to see them.

When we desire power other than the power we need, however, we end up seeing and viewing things in life differently from the way Father meant them to be. How many times, when we desire power other than the power God intended us to have, do we go back later complaining to Him that life just isn't working out? Learn to accept the amount of power that Father has chosen for you. If we become myopic, we may choose to want more power than we need. If we obtain too much power, that may allow us to end up with things we should not have desired. Too much power distorts our focus, and our view of life often becomes corrupted.

On the other hand, if we settle for far less power than what is available to us, we will never obtain all the clarity in life that Father desires for us. These self-imposed limits will prevent us from being able to do the greater things with our lives that God has planned for us to accomplish.

So, take a moment and ask yourself, how are things looking in your life? Are you seeing things through God's eyes? Have you chosen to receive the correct amount of power to have in your life? We should allow God to balance out the power we want with the power we need. Only then will we be able to see life as God intends for us to see it.

Chapter Sixty-Three
HUMBLE PIE

After I finished in an eye clinic one day, I decided to visit the squatter's village adjacent to a garbage dump. While I walked through the village I could not escape the overpowering stench and the sun's intense heat. There was no shelter to protect me. The mothers and fathers living there worked in this garbage dump every day, twelve hours a day, in the nearly unbearable heat.

The children's situation gripped my heart. Most of them were barefoot. All of them looked like they had not had a bath for many months. Some of them tried to help their parents find cardboard or scrap aluminum. They could sell these items to a scrap dealer. On a good day, a family may be able to earn around $1.25. Due to such poverty, I realized that those children would never get out of that barrio. Never! They would never have the possibility to escape or travel anywhere. Most had little or no education and their clothes were filthy and reeked. Even if they wanted to work, they would never find employment.

Later that evening I talked with Father. I had an avalanche of questions for Him.

"Why have you given those children a lifetime sentence of poverty? Why are they suffering? Is it because of their parents' poor choices? Why does a child have no hope for the future? Why does this scenario even exist?"

"It's all because you keep too much for yourself, Bryan," Father replied.

"No way, God, that can't be," I thought. "Why would you put that on me? You know everything I've done! I have names, Father, of people who keep too much for themselves. How many names would you like?"

I knew Father had spoken Truth again. If I was honest with myself, I still had an abundance of many things.

Sure, we had downsized our lifestyle and moved to a smaller home, but it was still large by the world's standards. We have spare bedrooms that we seldom use. We have nice cars to drive that are paid for. Our refrigerators, pantry, and closets are always full. We can cool or heat our home to whatever temperature we want it to be. I spend money on numerous comforts that billions of people on this planet do not. Father was teaching me that I have, in fact, still kept quite a lot for myself. I could do so much more than I was willing to do to help people out. I shamefully once again had to agree that He was correct.

FROM THAT TEACHING I LEARNED NOT TO USE OTHers as a barometer to measure my good works, or whether or not I kept too much or too little for myself. From then on, I learned to listen only to God's opinion of that.

My self-righteous bubble of pride popped when I realized why the children in that barrio suffered lifetime sentences of poverty. It is partly because of my own greed and desire to keep too much for myself. I knew I had to do more.

THREE YEARS LATER WITH THE HELP OF SOME amazing friends, God's Eyes bought a piece of land. We built a house for a family of six who formerly lived in a dilapidated shack in a garbage dump.

AFTER HELPING THAT FAMILY, I LEARNED A VERY important lesson: I can do more about the horrible conditions people are suffering in if I become willing to offer up more of what I keep. From time to time we should all ask Father this question. What is it I can do to help others and am I doing everything you want me to? I know that God will answer those prayers.

THEY SHALL SEE GOD

THE FAMOUS GOLFER, BOBBY JONES, ONCE PENAL-ized himself for accidentally moving his ball. No one else saw him do it. The golf media praised him for being so honest.

"Why would you praise me for doing something that you're supposed to do? " he asked them.

I, too, have received many undeserved accolades from people. They mistakenly believe that I am doing very special work and achieving great things. Father has taught me that I should never think I'm doing enough good or that I'm doing better things than others are doing, but rather to realize that at my very best, I'm only doing as Bobby said ...*what I'm supposed to do.*

"Why do you call me good? No one is good except for God." (Luke 18:19)

God's Eyes Warehouse with over 500,000 lenses in stock.

*76-year-old Felix with his first bible after
praying to receive Christ in Ecuador.*

〜

Chapter Sixty-Four

THE MAN WITH THE PIZZA SIGN

I remember my son calling me and asking me if I could play golf with him one morning. It was one of those miserably hot and muggy summer days in Atlanta, but I hadn't played a round of golf for a while, so I agreed to play. We brought along two half-gallon containers of ice-cold water and easily downed most of them before we had finished eighteen holes.

I dropped my son off at his home, then headed to God's Eyes headquarters. I knew I had a lot to get done that day and was running behind because I played golf.

As I drove home, in the distance I saw a man on the side of the road with a sign advertising a pizza parlor. The pizza parlor was in the shopping center behind where he was. He danced enthusiastically while juggling and spinning the small billboard.

I felt like the Lord wanted me to stop and give this guy the half-gallon container of the water that I had leftover from our golf game.

"Not today, Lord," I said. "I'm running behind and I've got a lot to do."

As I drove closer, the Lord nudged me again.

"Are you going to drive right by him?"

"Yes, please use someone else today to be a blessing for that guy. Besides, the water in the container is now kind of warm. Most of the ice has melted by now. And Lord, you know how much work I have to get finished today."

When my car sped by the guy spinning the pizza sign, I refused to look at him.

"You're not going to stop?" Father said.

"Nope!" again I told myself. "Too much work to do," and I drove on by.

I tried to put it out of my mind, but the thoughts would not go away. What if that was me standing outside in the hot sun? I sure would want some water to drink. I felt justified in not stopping, by telling myself that I had important work that needed to be finished.

"Lord, it's work I'm doing for you!"

I continued driving. About a mile down the road a stop light turned red just as I was about to drive through it. I was in a hurry, but I had to stop. I looked to my left and there was a Wendy's restaurant. I thought a nice ice-cold Wendy's shake sure sounded good.

But, how could I even think of stopping for myself, and not for the guy standing in the hot sun a mile back? I knew what Father wanted me to do and I finally surrendered. I pulled into Wendy's and ordered the largest chocolate shake they had.

"And also, I want the largest cup of ice that you can give me."

I then drove back to the guy holding the sign, parked nearby, and walked up to him.

"These are for you."

The guy was so glad. He was sweating profusely. I filled up the ice cup with water and gave it to him. He gulped it down. Then I handed him the chocolate milkshake.

"God must surely love you a lot because He wouldn't stop bothering me until I helped you."

Then something prompted me to find out if he knew anything about Jesus.

"Yep. Jesus lives right here," and he pointed to his heart.

I told him that I was proud of him for standing out there in the heat holding up that sign.

"Well, I *gots* to do this. I *gots* to make money somehow."

"No, you don't have to do this. Many people would just figure out some way to have the government support them instead of choosing to work. I'm proud of you for choosing to work hard, especially out in this heat."

I blessed him with the money I had left in my wallet. And I told him that Father loved him and was proud of him, too.

That day I learned how nice it feels to stop and do something kind for a stranger. We should think twice about driving past someone we could help just because we tell ourselves we have other important things to do. If I stop, that opens an opportunity for me to be the blessing Father wants me to be. I learned that we should not only "stop and smell the roses," but offer whatever help we can.

Here is another one of the hundreds of litmus tests in the Bible to see if we're acting like believers. 1 John 3:17 says, *"If anyone has material possessions and sees a brother or sister in need and does not have pity on them, how can the love of God be in them?"*

INSIDE OF ME IS A STILL SMALL VOICE, ENCOURAG-ing me to love others and consider them as important as myself. One of my great friends, Denny, says it best: *"We are to love more people and to love people more."*

AS I WAS WRITING THIS STORY, THE MAIL LADY RANG my doorbell. She had a certified letter that needed to be signed. I asked her how her day was going, and she answered, "It's fine but it's so hot out today."

As she walked away, I remembered what I just finished typing above. I ran to the kitchen and grabbed a cold bottle of water and took it out to her mail truck.

Slowly, very slowly, I am learning to love others.

◠◠

Chapter Sixty-Five
DID I CAUSE THAT?

During my fourth or fifth visit to Haiti, I was about to attend Saturday evening devotions when the director of services asked me if I would like to preach in church the next day. I had been telling Father for quite some time that I wanted to give the sermon in a church, but I meant in a church back in the States. What could I possibly talk to poor people about? I knew so little of their world. I told the director that I would pray about it during devotions and talk with her afterward. My real reason for saying that was so I could think of a good excuse not to do it. I didn't even ask Father what He wanted me to do. Instead, I had already made up my mind not to do it.

The next day the eye team had already planned to go to the Far West and do a small eye clinic and I didn't need to be there. They would have been fine without me as there were several eye doctors on that trip. However, I did want to go along with them. I decided I could use this as an excuse to get out of preaching. After devotions were over, I went up to the director and told her I would love to preach, but that I just couldn't because I had to be with the eye team that was going to the Far West.

She asked me if I was sure about that and I said yes.

Then she said, "That's odd because I've spent a long time praying about who should preach and I was positive that God told me you were supposed to."

I replied quite curtly "Well, I guess you were mistaken!"

EARLY THE NEXT DAY WE LEFT FOR OUR THREE-HOUR drive to the Far West. We planned to go to the village of La Baie to see forty patients. However, we ended up seeing ninety-seven instead. It took a few extra hours to get there because the dirt roads had turned into huge mud lakes. This was caused by a hurricane a few days before we arrived in Haiti. It dumped nineteen inches of rain on that region, therefore we got a late start to the clinic that day.

We were supposed to leave La Baie by four o'clock in the afternoon so that we would arrive back at the base camp by 7 p.m., before dark. It was already dark when we left and neither the bus nor the truck we traveled in had any working headlights. (They didn't need working headlights because no one in their right mind would ever be outside basecamp at night.) It's extremely dangerous to be out after dark in that desolate area of Haiti and of course, our bus got stuck in the mud on the way back...and I mean stuck as in, we couldn't budge it.

One of the missionaries from the base camp was with us and he phoned the head director of the mission and asked him to send some trucks to rescue us. He refused to send out any trucks. He said it would have been too dangerous to send more people out in the dark. I thought to myself that he had absolutely no concern for our lives, and I promised myself if I ever got back alive to the base, I would punch him in the face. (Can you feel the love radiating out of me?)

The base missionary then called some of his friends and they agreed to pick us up if we walked to the other side of the mud fields. If we did that they would drive us the rest of the way back to base. So, we had to abandon the vehicles and walk. We ended up walking for nearly an hour in the dark and through ankle-deep mud.

During that hike, I stepped into a deep mud hole. My right foot was impaled by large two-inch thorns that easily penetrated the rubber flip-flop sandals I was wearing. A few feet later I was impaled two more times. I walked the rest of the way through stagnant water and mud puddles with three puncture wounds in my right foot. This hike took place during one of the worst cholera outbreaks in Haitian history. As I walked, I prayed I wouldn't get sick and die but at least part of me believed I probably would. We were quite a sight. Thirty white people were tromping through these mud roads in the dark.

I was amazed that some of the people in our group sang worship songs to Father as they endured the walk. I didn't. This relative newbie missionary grumbled nonstop to God during the entire walk. We finally made it through the mud fields and 30 of us piled into the truck beds of the three small pick-up trucks. After a rather terrifying ride during which we were almost attacked, we arrived at base camp close to midnight. That part of the story is for another time.

That night I was too upset to sleep and I realized there was a definite similarity between the story of Jonah and my story. Neither of us did what the Lord wanted us to and both of us went somewhere else instead. In the story of Jonah, he was the cause of much suffering for others and I began to feel the whole mud field thing may have been my fault. I immediately repented and told Father if He ever wanted me to preach at a church in the future I would say yes immediately! I never wanted to go through anything like that again or put anyone else through that either.

Chapter Sixty-Six
MOVING

God's Eyes had only been in its first headquarters for three years when our landlord said he was not going to renew our lease. He had decided he wanted to use the space for himself, and he planned on moving his real estate office into the space we were renting. We only had a few months to find a new location. It was going to be difficult because he had been leasing this space to us for well below the going rate.

During those next few months, I was also scheduled to be on several mission trips. This didn't leave me a whole lot of time to find a new location and get everything moved. It felt like it might be impossible with limited time and a small budget. By this time, though, I was learning about the power of prayer. So that's what I did. I started praying about where we might move our headquarters.

Even if I doubled the budget for rent, there was nothing available anywhere near that price. Our rent was only $600 per month. The cheapest space I could find was $1500 per month and those units were in terrible shape. One such place was a smelly old auto mechanics garage that was a total mess. I knew the cheapest spaces would be found in an old warehouse rental area a few miles away from our current space. Still, they were all renting for too much and they were all old and dingy.

A friend told me I could use a part of his plumbing supply warehouse to store our supplies for free, but it was over an hour away. In addition, we would still have to rent office space so we could set up and operate the optical lab. Things weren't looking so good, but I trusted that God would supply a place for the new headquarters. Surprisingly, I wasn't as worried as I normally would be.

I called a former patient of mine who owned a commercial real estate business. He asked me what my maximum budget was. I told him $1500 per month. In the back of my mind, I didn't know how God's Eyes could even afford that amount. He said he didn't think there would be much of anything available for that price, and I knew he was right. He showed me some properties that were too expensive or were so old that they would require too much additional money to modify for our needs. The deal we had been given for the previous three years was unheard of.

Two miles from my home, a brand-new office/warehouse park had just been completed. A former patient of mine had his name on the sign as the leasing agent. I asked him about the new buildings.

"Forget about those units, they are way more expensive than your budget can afford," he said.

A few days later he showed me some older and dilapidated properties.

"Sorry but that's all that's available anywhere near your budget."

That same day we got stuck at a railroad crossing as a train started to go through the crossing. Then it stopped altogether, preventing us from getting through. Both of us had busy days planned and we needed to get back to our offices, but the train sat there blocking our ability to cross the tracks for over an hour. During that time, we chatted, and I began to tell him stories of what God was doing through God's Eyes and stories about the places I had been to.

When the tracks finally cleared, we moved on.

"How old are you, Bryan?"

"I'm fifty-three."

"And how much longer are you going to keep up this crazy schedule of traveling all around the world? What do you think you have left in you, maybe five to eight years before you retire?"

"I plan on doing this for the rest of my life."

He was silent for a minute.

"Ok, since you answered that way, let's go look at those new warehouses by your home."

I guess he figured we were both so far behind in what we had scheduled for the day that another hour wasn't going to make any difference. The new office and warehouses were amazing. There was a great spot for the optical lab with a large warehouse connected to it. The space was four times the size of where we were.

There was only one problem: the cost.

"I know your budget is only $1,500 per month so let me talk it over with the guy who owns the property."

"If it's at all possible I'd also prefer a long-term lease. I want to be locked in for at least five years."

"Bryan, that's probably never going to happen, but I'll get back to you."

I started praying even more now. I thought this space would be perfect if God could make it happen. Then I started to worry a little bit because even if he could get it for the price I told him, I wasn't sure we could afford it.

The next day he called me.

"You're not going to believe this, but I told the owner what you did and why you needed the space, and he made a great offer! Two years at $1,200 per month and then $1,250 for the third year, $1,300 for the fourth year, and $1,350 for the fifth year!"

Wow! Not only did he go for a long-term lease, but he also did it for even less than what we were hoping. I told him to give me a couple of days so I could pray about it and that I would call him back. I think he thought I was crazy not to accept the offer on the spot. He said, ok, but that I had better make up my mind fast.

I knew it was an amazing offer, but I had learned by this time to run everything through God first. Remember the whole story about common sense versus God sense? Besides, I didn't even know how we would ever go from $600 per month to the $1,200 per month he offered. That night I asked

God if I should accept the offer and, if I did, would He provide the additional $600 a month in rent money. As I had previously learned to do, I prayed the following, "God if you want me to do this, please confirm it."

The very next day a dear long-time donor called me out of the blue.

"Bryan, I've been donating to God's Eyes for a few years now. Every time you go on a God's Eyes mission trip God uses it to increase His kingdom. I feel like God is telling me to increase my support by an extra $600 per month starting this month."

Well, that was the confirmation I needed from Father to sign the new rental agreement, and I did. Even before we moved into our new headquarters God had supplied the money we needed for the rent increase. I smiled. I was learning, on an ever-increasing basis, that at least some of the time things work out when you trust in God.

Chapter Sixty-Seven
STAY WITH ME

One day while I was praying, Father interrupted me.

"I need to correct you."

"What am I doing wrong?" I asked Him.

"You are teaching people to come to me whenever they have a question, a need, or desire a situation to be changed. Sometimes you teach them to come to me when they want healing for themselves or others, or numerous other reasons."

"Yes, I am, Father. That's exactly what I do. I do tell people to call upon you."

"That's not my desire. I don't want people to hop in and out with me, only coming to me when they need or want something. I want them to stay with me."

Immediately I had two thoughts or visions, or whatever you choose to call them.

The first one was of a young couple, perhaps in their early twenties, who are in love with each other. They experience great joy while together. One night one of them travels to the other's house. They have dinner together and spend time snuggled up against each other while watching a movie. As the evening goes on, one says they have to leave.

"I must go now."

"No, don't go!" says the other one. "I don't want you to leave, just stay here with me."

That's how I believe Father feels about us. He doesn't want us to leave His presence. He loves us. He wants us to stay with Him. He wants us to want to be with Him.

The second "vision" was of a very old couple who had been married for many, many years. They are perhaps in their eighties or nineties. They are together, but he is now on his deathbed. She is sitting beside him holding his hand and brushing her fingers through his hair. She kisses him on his forehead. In a moment, he will die, and she knows it. She cries out.

"Please don't go. Stay! Stay with me for just another five minutes, please, just ten more minutes. Please! "

THAT IS HOW I ALSO BELIEVE FATHER FEELS TOWARDS us. He doesn't need us. He just desires us. He is the lover of our souls and wants to be with us. He longs for intimacy with us. He doesn't want us to just call His name only when we have a need and then disappear. He not only loves us, but He is Love itself! We should move into His arms and remain there reciprocating the love He offers us. If we want to be holy, then we must give time to God and not just intend to do so.

We need to move in with Him permanently and stop being just visitors!

Psalm 91:4 teaches us that

"He will cover you with his wings, you'll be safe in his care, His faithfulness will protect and defend you."

Why would we want to be anywhere else?

Chapter Sixty-Eight

PLANS I HAVE FOR YOU

When I give talks, I often quote Ephesians 2:10:
"We are God's workmanship, created in Christ Jesus to do good works, which God has prepared in advance for us to do."

The first four words are spectacular! We are God's workmanship! Letting that sink in feels terrific. We are his workmanship! We are something special! I OFTEN THINK OF MICHELANGELO WHEN I DWELL on those four words. Michelangelo carved the Pietà when he was only 24 years old. It remains today as one of the most magnificent works of art ever made. He miraculously transformed a giant lump of granite into an artistic masterpiece by carving away the part of the rock he didn't need. For the rest of his life, Michelangelo could look back at what he created from a single piece of marble and admire what he accomplished. The Pietà is worthy of that admiration and so is the incredible skill that its maker possessed. For centuries people have traveled from all over the world to gaze at his creation. It was Michelangelo's workmanship, and it is spectacular.

In much the same way, we are Father's workmanship. What the Lord has made is infinitely more spectacular than we can imagine. He admires us and He is pleased with what He has made. We are a living piece of art that

*Sometimes there are no buildings to hold God's Eyes clinics,
so we work outside instead.*

*The famous "Woody" wearing "The Woody" T-shirt.
He promotes God's Eyes wherever he goes.*

Father sculpted. We are His, His workmanship. If we ever feel unimportant or worthless, we should just take a moment to realize just how magnificent a creation we really are.

The rest of the verse is also inspiring. *"We were created in Christ Jesus to do good works which He has prepared in advance for us to do."*

WHICH GOOD WORKS ARE WE TO DO? THE ONES HE "prepared in advance" for us to do. Yes, Father made us. We are beautiful and important to Him. We were created to do specific good works. We have a purpose.

If you know me you've heard me say this before, but it bears repeating if not memorizing. In the book of Jeremiah, chapter 33, verse 3, the Lord gives us His advice and a promise:

"Call on me and I WILL answer you and I will tell you great and hidden things you do not know."

THERE IT IS. IT'S JUST THAT SIMPLE. WE MUST CALL on Him. We must ask and seek and listen to Father as to what we are to do. When we call on Him, He will answer us. It is a promise He gives us! He always keeps His promises. And what will He do when He answers? He will tell us great and hidden things we do not know. Things like what good works He has prepared in advance for us to do, or even more things that we need to learn. He will reveal things we do not even know enough to ask about.

Earlier in the book of Jeremiah, in chapter 29, verse 11, it says:

"I know the plans I have for you, says the Lord, plans to prosper you, not to harm you, plans to give you hope and a future."

HE HAS PLANS FOR US AND THEY ARE NOT TO HARM us. If Father desires not to harm us, then we shouldn't blame Him if harm does befall us. That was not from Him. His plans are to give us hope and a future.

GOD IS LOOKING FOR PEOPLE THROUGH WHOM HE can do the impossible. What a pity if what we plan are only simple tasks that we can accomplish on our own. So, let's call on Father and listen to His revelations. Let's find out what good works He has prepared for us to do. Let's discover our hope and learn what our future is meant to be.

Chapter Sixty-Nine
MY HOPE

God's Eyes has helped many people throughout the world, but no matter what the final number equals one day, the correct answer will always be that we have not helped enough! At nearly every clinic we have ever held we have had to turn people away because there are too many of them and not enough of us. Somedays I felt that we turned away more people than we helped. This was always the part of a trip that I hated the most. After standing in the heat or rain all day some of them would have to go back from where they came with nothing but an additional dose of disappointment. I have had people on their knees with their arms wrapped around my legs begging me to help their child or parent before I left. I sometimes would run to the bus or truck when I was getting ready to leave or I would hide behind a building and cry as their pleading and tears caused my own heart to be ripped apart.

As I've previously written, on one hand, this journey that started a decade and a half ago has literally been the most heart-wrenching thing I've ever experienced. However, this journey has also produced some of the best moments I have ever encountered. My wife Jenn and I frequently say that we are no longer rich, but we are wealthy. This path led us to discover an intimacy with Father that we had not known or had even heard about in church. His love for us IS immeasurable and I long for you to experience it if you have not.

I have traveled to some faraway places. Most were to towns or villages, I'd never heard of before. I traveled there on roads I never knew existed, while on my journey of bringing vision to the world.

This is a little of what I've learned. There is an incredible amount of suffering in this world. There is terrible and horrific suffering along with injustices that are so numerous that perhaps they cannot even be counted. However, you and I can do something about that. Some of us can help a little and others can help more but no matter who we are, all of us are capable of alleviating somebody's pain to some extent. All of you play an important part in the Body of Christ and are desired greatly.

SADLY, I HAVE MET THOSE WHO ARE DISCOURAGED about the contribution that their lives can give to this world and God. There is an old African proverb that states, "If you think you're too small to make a difference, you haven't spent the night in a tent with a mosquito." I speak from experience and believe me, a single mosquito can make a difference in a very annoying way. However, the principle remains the same. No matter how insignificant you feel, don't believe for a minute that you have nothing to offer to improve this world.

I STARTED THIS JOURNEY QUITE SOME TIME AGO. AS I'm sure you've ascertained by now, I was reluctant to begin. There have been many times when I wanted to not only veer off this path but to run in a different direction. However, along the way as I eventually learned to stay the course, some of my reluctance gradually changed to obedience, and joy began to replace fear and doubt. I now love, better, easier, and more generously than I did before this journey started. It's hard to explain but when I allow it to happen, an abundance of peace fills my heart and mind and the presence of Father always seems close by. That's truly an amazing, and wonderful thing to experience.

THEY SHALL SEE GOD

IT'S DIFFICULT TO CONDENSE ONE'S LIFE INTO A book. I have written and rewritten this one more times than I care to remember. Many stories and lessons I've learned along the way have not made the cut. My friends tell me they are all meant for a second or third book. However, I'm not sure I like those suggestions as I much prefer speaking to writing. I can only hope that the stories included in this book have shed some light on the twists and turns encountered by imperfect, and former reluctant missionaries like me.

AFTER READING THIS BOOK I HOPE THAT YOU WILL be inspired to "run the good race" and go for the trophy that will never rust. That you and others will be compelled to serve Him in all circumstances, both difficult and easy, and in all ways, both simple and great. Everything we do in accordance with His will pleases Father greatly and is of eternal value. Please choose wisely, walk through the narrow gate, taking the road that is less traveled, whose way is difficult but leads to everlasting life.

MY FINAL WISH IS THAT YOUR PERSONAL JOURNEY will lead you to love more people and that you fall in love with the One who loves you. Realize when God looks at you He doesn't care: what denomination you belong to, your political affiliation, what language you speak, the color of your skin, how attractive or intelligent you are, how many degrees you've earned, or the amount of riches you've accumulated.

HE SEES ONLY YOUR SOUL, WHICH HE LOVES WITH unending passion. He fights hard for it. Our souls are so important to Him that He sent His Son to die so they may be set free. Every time you look at someone, look at them the way Father does. See only their soul and love it the way He does. I pray that one day we will all learn to see everything the way we were meant to see, through God's Eyes.

LETTERS OR DONATIONS BY CHECK
God's Eyes US Headquarters:
825 Highway 74 South
Suite 105
Peachtree City, Georgia, 30269

BRING BRYAN TO YOUR EVENT
Bryan is a sought after speaker for conferences, churches, and
small groups, inspiring people to "Take The Leap". Whether
a live event or virtual, Bryan would love to come and bring
his unique blend of storytelling, humor, wit, and wisdom.
www.godseyes.com/speak

EXPERIENCE GOD'S EYES
If you would like to go on a mission trip or learn more about
God's Eyes mission of bringing vision to the world.
www.godseyes.com

 GOD'S EYES

CPSIA information can be obtained
at www.ICGtesting.com
Printed in the USA
LVHW082255070922
727851LV00015B/1170

9 798885 906418